He makes beauty out of ashes

Dear Broken Girl...

ALEXIS HOWELL

Cover illustration by Ashley Howell (my sissy)

MY LOVES

"I am so thankful for you. You're supportive, loyal, kind, loving, goofy, and protective. You have given me so much advice and it has never steered me wrong. I don't know if I ever told you this, but I hope that one day I can be just as close to God as you are. I want to be just like you in every way. When you're around, you have a positive glow that just makes me smile. Omg sis, I love you so much!"

Lil 'sis', Audrey Ives
Selma, NC

"Lexi, I sit here and think of the wonderful young person you are and can't wait to see what God has in store for you. God is a wonderful leader and we must all rely on Him to give us guidance, love, assurance, and feeling of grace. He is looking ahead to keep us safe and in what will He has planned for us. We must allow Him to work in our lives on His time, not ours. God is willing to work through and out any storms that we face. Remember to always put God first and everything else will fall into place. God cares for you and wants what is best for His sheep. Remember, trust in God's unfailing love for ever and ever (Psalm 52:8). I love you!"

Michelle Moore
Princeton, NC

"You hold within your hands a special treasure – 'DEAR BROKEN GIRL' by Alexis M. Howell. As a 60+ year old grandmother who carries scars from her teen years… I would've loved to have had the opportunity to read the truths contained within Lexi's book. You will relate with her struggles, rejoice with her victories, but most of all, you will rehearse its content, your view of self will be renewed. Lexi takes off her mask, is genuine and vulnerable, for you to know that *you were made for more*."

Sylvia Wolfe
Smithfield, NC

"Lexi is an extraordinary person who has a perspective on life and God that will change culture for years to come. She is an inspiration to everyone that wants to leave the mark of grace on the world. Lexi just doesn't talk about change, she lives it. I have watched God take a broken and wounded young girl and grow her into a vibrant instrument of love, grace and change. Everyone who has an interaction with Lexi is better because of it. I am excited to see how God will continue to use her to move the world back to His heart"

Pastor Scooter Murphy
Princeton, NC

"Every teenage girl should have a personal copy of 'Dear Broken Girl'. The teenage author, Lexi Howell wrote the book in a funny conversational style that will make her every girl's BFF. This is a brilliant life changing guide for any young person who wants to live for Jesus."

Doris Anderson Sanders
Spring, TX

"Tootsie roll, it is a pleasure and honor to be your big sister and to watch you grow up from a goofy kid to a goofy young woman of God. Your love for Christ and the hearts of people is unmatched and I am beyond blessed that God entrusted our family to have you. You are a true blessing to so many others and I cannot wait until your truth in this book is shared with the world so that those who are broken can know that there is power and healing in our Creator, our Father, Christ Jesus. You never cease to amaze me and I am beyond excited to see what God has in store for your future. I love you beyond any measure of words."

Ashley Howell (Snickers)
Richmond, VA

"Alexis, you were born with a heart of love; a bundle of compassion to help the broken. We pray over you God's blessings and success in all that you do. Know that we are so proud of you for not only adhering to God and writing this book but for your walk and talk with God. You have grown into a beautiful young woman of God and we are looking forward to seeing what God's future holds for you! May God continue to be your guide and your protection as He directs your steps.

Mommy and daddy

For we are God's masterpiece. He has created us anew in Christ Jesus, so we can do the good things he planned for us long ago.

-Ephesians 2:10 NLT

"Such an inspiration from one so young.

Thanks author Alexis Howell. You have a title."

- Mrs. Mary 'Libby' Howell Whitley
  Selma, NC

Prophetic words spoken in 2015

Although you are not here to see His promises being fulfilled, I know you are smiling and praising God from above.

Rest in Peace sweet angel – Mary Howell Whitley (December 2016)

So shall My word be that goes forth from My mouth; It shall not return to Me void,
But it shall accomplish what I please,
And it shall prosper in the thing for which I sent it.
-Isaiah 55:11

Dear Broken Girl...

...you are made for more

A poem of love dedicated to my mom,

Mira Howell

Dear Mom,
Where do I begin?
From the time I was born until now you have
been my very best friend.
No words can express, nor actions can be shown
How much for you my love has grown
Mom, your love is extraordinary
You, mom, are definitely not ordinary!
Oh, how you worship and sing praise
What great honor it fully displays!
The joy that you bring me cannot be fathomed
You are more to me than
I have ever hoped or imagined.
There are times we have our mini fights
but it never stops us from saying,
"I love you" at night.
Your genuine heart is so amazing,
I can't even explain.
Mommy, my love for you will
forever and ever remain!

CHAPTERS

One: Who you are //

- Remember the truth, remove the lies … 2

- Rejection … 7

- Pursued … 10

- The flu attacks the body; the devil attacks the mind … 12

- Your life has changed … 17

- Obedience … 21

Two: Dear broken girl //

- Shift your perspective … 31

- Small moves make huge impacts … 35

- It's the same blood … 36

- You're never too far gone to come home … 39

- Who is this Man? … 43

- He's a good, good Father … 51

- Broken to broken … 52

- Falling at the feet of Jesus … 55

- Dear broken girl, it's time to fight back … 59

Three: I'd rather be single //

- Temptation … 67

- Total surrender to God … 70

- Will I be single forever, God? … 71

- Who you are … 76

- Set boundaries … 77

- Promise ring … 80

- Don't date just to pass the time … 81

- What are you connected to? … 85

- A date with my heavenly Father … 89

- Boyfriend wanted – not needed … 92

Four: Yeah, me too //

- ◆ The freedom only He brings … 96

- ◆ Money, money, money … 100

- ◆ Valleys, trials and defeat – oh my! … 104

- ◆ God, this is how I feel … 105

- ◆ Who's on the throne of your heart … 109

- ◆ Boy crazy … 113

Five: Willingness in the waiting //

- ◆ Waiting on God … 116

- ◆ Faithfulness … 122

- ◆ Goals … 127

- ◆ Choose a leader … 131

- ◆ Dear future husband … 133

- ◆ Trust without borders … 135

- ◆ Dear broken girl … 140

<u>LOVE DEDICATION:</u>

To my main Man (Jesus), thank You for making me so wonderfully complex! Thank You for even considering that the world needed one of me in it. Thank You for Your love and pursuit of me! You are my everything! Use me for Your glory! Lord, I'm Yours. Do what You want to!!

Love You forever!

To my twin, my daddy, the one and only Keith Howell, thank you for the strong genes and the encouraging words. Thank you for the love and hugs that you give me. You are the first man I have ever loved, and I couldn't think of a better person to become my first love. I've watched the Lord shape you into such an awesome man of God. I will forever be your little girl.

I love you daddy!

Ashley, my sissy... my snickers! We may have an eight-year age difference, but as we grow into mature adults the joy and laughs that we share brings us closer together. Thank you for showing me the latest trends and for not only being my sister but my favorite friend.

Love you bunches!

To my mema, my boo, my girl, you and I have so much in common – it's scary! You've sacrificed so much for me. From quitting your job to take care of me so that I wouldn't have to go to daycare; to driving me to school every day until I was able to drive myself. You are our cook, our doctor without a license, our advisor without us asking, our fashion designer even though you can't match colors. You, mema are the backbone of our family. I love you so much and I'm grateful to have such a sassy, yet hard-working, tender loving mema like you. There is no one like you *(thank God)* and I will forever love you!

Annie Libert, regardless of what the others say, I am your #1 baby!

Love you boo!

To my church, you have molded me into the lady that I am! Six years ago, when my family and I walked into your home… that's exactly what it felt like – home! Because of your love and willingness to work with my spiritual man, I'm better because of it! Thank you, Temple of Selma NC!

"Representing Christ Well"

Last but not least…

I would like to send out a special *"thank you"* to:

- Doris Anderson Sanders
- Sylvia Wolfe
- Michelle Moore
- Pastor Frances Shepherd
- Mira Howell (mommy)

for your spiritual guidance as well as your words of encouragement during the development of Dear Broken Girl. I love you guys!

Chapter 1

WHO YOU ARE

"Your beauty should not come from outward
adornment, such as elaborate hairstyles and the
wearing of gold jewelry or fine clothes. Rather, it
should be that of your inner self, the unfading beauty
of a gentle and quiet spirit, which is of great worth
in God's sight."

– 1 Peter 3:3-4

Remember the truth, remove the lies

[True Life Moment #1] This is a real-life mind battle moment that I faced but God conquered

Lexi, you're not as pretty as they are! I mean just look at you! Lose the glasses, put in some contacts! He'll never like you because you don't look like that other girl! Your crush overlooks you because of your race! You don't have white teeth or a butt like hers! Get it together, would you? You don't measure up! You never have and you never will! Your laugh is ridiculous and so are you! You're too "Christian", loosen up! You desire to be liked by everyone, right? Well, then get on their level and do what they do! Wear makeup to cover up what they don't like! Obviously, if you made yourself look better, then guys would pursue you and think you're beautiful! Your beauty needs work!" – **Satan**

Wow! Satan truly attacks the most crucial thing to us — our minds. He targets and manipulates how we picture ourselves. I'm thankful for a Father who reminds us of our *true* worth. God sees us as beautiful, and now it's time for us to do the same. We are not worthless! We are loved, seen, beautiful and most importantly wanted by God (right where we are)!

He makes beauty
from ashes

"You're not smart enough"   "You're too fat"

"You're not pretty enough"

"You're too skinny"   "You don't measure up"

"You're not enough"

"You're all alone"   "You're worthless"

"You're ugly"

"You're not loved"   "Your life doesn't matter"

ENOUGH IS ENOUGH!

It's time to take back what the devil has stolen from us!! And now, let's replace it with what the Lord says about us!

YOU are set apart!   **YOU are fearless!**

YOU are forgiven!   **YOU are a princess!**

YOU are chosen!   **YOU are seen!**

YOU are accepted!   **YOU matter!**

YOU have a purpose!   **YOU are wanted!**

Let these truths wash over you today and bask in the glory of our good, good Father!

Understand this - you are wonderfully complex! Unlike any other! Unique! Different! *Set apart, not set aside.* You are cherished and adored by the King of kings and Lord of lords. He believes in you and He sees you for who you truly are. He loves you just as you are with all your blemishes, stains, and *sin*. Jesus replaces what the devil, society and even you say about yourself. Brokenness is labeled as whole in His Book. You see ugly, but in His eyes you are stunning. You see an unlovable being, yet He Himself who is love desires to wrap you in His gracious arms and whisper what every girl wants to hear, "I love you. The real you. The messed-up parts, the good, the bad and the ugly - all of you!" Jesus is SO in-love with us that He *willingly* meets us right where we are.

You're beautiful. **Believe** it.

You're loved. **Receive** it.

You have a purpose. **Live** it.

Most importantly, when you stumble, fall or simply ignore Him because you choose to listen to Satan's lies, He is *still* with you. Patiently waiting! Jesus sticks by our side because to Him we are worth the nails, crown of thorns and gashes of open wounds! We are expensive! We were bought at a high price in which no one other than Jesus can ever repay.

Abba Father,

Thank You for pursuing me... because to You, Abba, I am worth the pursuit. I love You.

Amen.

REJECTION

Fearful of being rejected?

Rejection. A word that floods our minds with bad experiences, unwanted feelings and many lies. Rejection shows up in our lives in many ways: when the college you applied to rejects you - you feel inadequate; the job that you interviewed for hires someone else – you feel defeated; you finally mustered up the courage to tell your crush that you liked him only to be told that the feeling isn't mutual. There are times it may even seem that the Lord has rejected you as well. *Dear Broken Girl,* God will never leave you nor forsake you. *(Hebrews 13:5)* It's during these moments that we have to remember, rejection by man is just a way to shift your focus of seeing your acceptance in Christ. Yes, it hurts to experience rejection by anyone for anything, but oh, how beautiful it is to know that you have been accepted by Christ! Remember, not everyone will like you. Some people will hate you simply because you are you. The same happened and still happens to Christ (*John 15:18-19*). Why? Because you're living for Someone they (the world) can't categorize or comprehend. I had to learn this the hard way. I always thought I was liked by everyone, but I soon came to realize that some people just didn't like me for no reason at all! This was a difficult pill to swallow and of course I questioned, "What did *I* do wrong?" I quickly learned that, for the most part, I didn't do anything wrong. Simply me breathing seemed to be a reason not to like me. I re-examined myself to see if I did or said anything that was inappropriate or unjust. Most importantly, I prayed to the Father for Him to examine my heart. After the heart-check and prayer, I understood that some people don't like me because of the Spirit that lives within me. The Lord warned us saying that

The opinions of others mean nothing compared to the promises of God.

following Him wouldn't be easy, but He did promise that He would be with us always. (*John 16:33; Matt. 28:20b*) The opinions of others mean nothing compared to the promises of God. We're not made to meet man's criteria, but we are made to fulfill the plans of God.

"The world would love you as one of its own if you belonged to it, but you are no longer part of the world. I chose you to come out of the world, so [that is why] it hates you."

- ***John 15:19***

God,

May I never forget that though man may reject me, You always accept me. Help me to find freedom in Your truths, pursuit and acceptance of me! I love You!
Amen.

PURSUED

Are you pursued by many guys or are you one to not be pursued? The amount of times you are pursued or not pursued by a guy does not determine your worth or validate your beauty. Your worth and beauty is in something far Greater. Don't believe me? Read *Psalm 139:1-4*. Dear Broken Girl, what truly matters is this truth: **you're pursued by the King**. You're not beautiful because someone likes you; you are beautiful because God created you.

You're not beautiful because someone likes you; you are beautiful because God created you.

I had a friend come to me one day all giddy about this new guy she was seeing. She told me all about her relationship, how long they've been together, how many dates they've been on, and she even showed me pictures of her new guy! Everything seemed to be going well for her, but I had a different outlook on this relationship. In one of our conversations, she explained how they had made plans to hang out, but it was cold outside. So, they decided to hang in his car instead. I asked, "Well, what did you guys do in the car?" She hesitated, and in that moment... I felt my Spirit sink. She finally answered in a quiet tone, "...We just made out a little." I knew my facial expression told her exactly what I was thinking. She then added, "It's not a big deal, Lexi." I responded, "Actually, it is." She doesn't know. She doesn't see in herself, what I see in her! I see a purpose that has been written deep within her heart by the King of kings. A worth that is far greater than what she's been settling for. I can see it clearly in her because the Lord revealed the same thing to me about myself. I used to have the same mindset as she did, as most girls do. I was so consumed by a guy, and because I was so consumed, I missed several red flags - the big "no-no's" if you will. Dear Broken Girl, our purpose is not found in a guy or our relationship status; our purpose and potential is wrapped in the fullness of God's grace.

The flu attacks the body; the devil attacks the mind

The devil deceives us by planting toxic seeds in our minds of not being "good enough". He tells us that we're fat, ugly, too tall, too short, insignificant, worthless, etc. The devil floods our minds with bad things (lies) just like the flu virus floods our body with toxins. With the flu you get aches, headaches and pains of the body. With the lies of Satan, you get aches, headaches, and pains of the mind. The devil and his lies are deadly, just like the flu. The flu kills many and has no respect of ethnicity, age or gender. It's the same thing with Satan. He doesn't care if you're 15, 26, or 47; African American, Caucasian, Asian, Hispanic, male or female, etc. His sole purpose is to attack our mind with toxic poison because he knows that within each of us is planted a seed of purpose. The devil knows the potential of what we can do for God and most importantly what God can do through us, ultimately leaving the devil defeated once again. *John 10:10* explains it perfectly when it says, *"The devil comes to steal, kill, and destroy…"* Did you get that? The devil and the flu are one in the same if you think about it. No one wants the flu, and if you happen to get the virus, you try to find a cure for it. It's the same with the poison that's planted by the devil. This can only be cured through Christ.

Dear Broken Girl, you may feel unlovable, but just in case you didn't know, over 2,000 years ago a perfect Man who knew NO sin took *our* sins and nailed it to the cross with His body. He was then resurrected holding victory in His hands with a desire to live within all those who freely accept Him! It wasn't the nails that held Jesus there. He could've easily told the Lord to end His suffering and the angels would've swooped down from Heaven to save Him. No, nails didn't keep Him on the cross. It was LOVE! Jesus loves us so much that He endured the pain, shame and suffering on the cross.

To those who feel worthless, you're not alone. Everyone gets to *that* place, but I encourage you to not stay in *that* place. For you have been called for more! I understand the darkness that worthlessness can bring. However, there is freedom! You are worth so much more than what others say or don't say about you. You are worth more than the grades you get compared to others. You are worth more than just losing your virginity to anyone that whispers, "I love you" and yet he doesn't even know your middle name. ****mic drop****

Purity - the condition or quality of being pure; freedom from anything that debases, contaminates, pollutes, etc.

Purity is such a beautiful thing, and once we somehow let darkness overshadow that, you're left with brokenness. *1 Thessalonians 4:3* reminds us that, *"God's will is for you to be holy, so stay away from all sexual sin"*.

There is so much joy, freedom, and love in Christ. I'm very thankful to be His daughter and to have an intimate relationship with Him. Yet, so many people in this world don't know that feeling. And maybe you, yourself have no idea of the joy and love that comes from God. Jesus tells us that in Him and in His presence, there is life. Many are roaming the earth spiritually "dead". The Word of God clearly states that we were not made to be "dead", but to have LIFE! A life that can only be found in Christ. The second part of *John 10:10* says, *"... but I have come so that you may have life and life more abundantly."*

There comes a time in each of our lives that we need to get to know ourselves (what's been spoken over us; identity) and who Jesus is to us personally. Take this season — whatever that season may be — and use it to further the Kingdom of God. How? Serve your community! Help that mother who works two jobs by volunteering to babysit her children some nights. Serve in a church that is rooted in the foundation of Christ. Take time out of your busy life and listen to the voice of God and then take it one step further and obey that voice. For some of you this may mean going on a missions trip out of the country and serving there, for others it may mean to serve in an area or organization within your church faithfully. It could mean being a light for other young women and girls around you as you proclaim the name of Jesus! Whatever you do, do it all for the glory of God!

God,
I'm Yours! Do what You want to! I am Your vessel! Prune, mold and purify me into the image You have set before me! I love You!
Amen.

Your life has changed

Most of us have heard the story of Saul. If you haven't, *(I encourage you to read the entire Book of Acts to get a better understanding of the story of Stephen and Saul)* but until then, let me give you a synopsis of Saul's life. Saul was an evil man who desired to kill all Christians. My story begins in *Acts 7* where Stephen, a man full of God's grace and power is destined to be stoned. In *Acts 7:58*, scripture says that as Stephen was being dragged out of the city and stoned, that there were witnesses who were placing their coats at the feet of a young man named Saul. What does this tell me? (1) That Saul had authority and (2) he was in complete agreement with this atrocious act of killing Stephen. (See *Acts 8:1*)

In Acts Chapter 9, we meet Saul once again. He is on his way to Damascus to imprison the Lord's people (men, women and children). Does this sound like someone else we've heard of? *John 10:10* says that *"the thief (Satan) comes only to steal, kill and destroy."* (Now stay with me ok, it gets long BUT I promise it's so worth it). While on the road to Damascus, God meets Saul *right where he is* (I love this because it means that God will accept me right where I am. I don't have to get everything in order first. I don't have to stop this or stop that first...... I simply have to be willing to hear God's voice). Let's continue. The Bible tells us that a light from Heaven flashed around Saul and the voice of the Lord spoke to him (*Acts 9:3*) basically wanting to know why Saul was persecuting His name. The Lord instantly made Saul blind. Then Saul was ordered to '*get up and go*' to Damascus. There were two men with Saul that had to help him get there because of his blindness. (How many of you know that when God reveals Himself to us, He could also reveal Himself to another individual that He wants to use to help us?) This is exactly what happened in Saul's story. While Saul is on his way to Damascus, the Lord reveals himself to a man by the name of Ananias in a dream, telling him to go and meet Saul. There are a couple things we need to keep in mind – (1) Saul is well known throughout the nation for killing Christians; and (2) Ananias was a Prophet aka he was a Christian. Ananias responded, *"Lord, I have heard many reports about this man and all the harm he has done to Your holy people in Jerusalem." (Acts 9:13)* Ananias was skeptical, as any normal Christian would be.

However, the Lord's response is one of my absolute favorites, He says, "Go! This man is my *chosen* instrument to proclaim My name." *(Acts 9:15)* WOW! Aren't you grateful for a Father who loves us enough that He doesn't leave us as we are… where we are, but is willing and able to mold us into what He has called us to be? Once Saul's eyes are open and He accepts Christ, his life is changed. He is no longer the Saul who persecuted God's people, but he is now a great warrior for Christ. No longer was he bound by his sins and mistakes. The Lord had given him a new life and purpose – to proclaim the Name he once persecuted. It is the same with us. We were born sinful, but we have been given the opportunity to not stay or remain in our sin. We have a choice to either continue to live our lives as persecutors of Christ or allow God to change our lives and become warriors of Christ. We can go from worthless to full of worth, lonely to never alone, messed up to masterpieces. Oh Dear Broken Girl, has your life been changed?

The world can't move you because you're rooted in Someone who is immovable.

OBEDIENCE

One night, I remember hearing God speak to me:

"What do you like to do, Lex?" — God

"I like to write."

"Now, go!" — God

In that same moment, I began to write. The presence of God was like I've never experienced before. Every word I had written that night I knew the Lord had spoken through me.

So, my question and challenge for you today is, what is the Lord calling you to do? Write that book; sing that song; love that student that everyone avoids or laughs at or perhaps it's simply volunteering. I encourage you, to do that 'thing' that you know the Lord has placed on your heart. Obedience to God may not be easy. It may be out of your comfort zone, but we have to remember that this is not about us; it's about God using us to not only open up doors for us but others.

Here's an example of 2 people who walked in obedience to the Lord:

1. **NOAH**
   - Found favor with the Lord because of his obedience
   - Walked in close fellowship with God
     - Noah knew God's voice and God knew Noah's voice
   - Was given instructions on <u>what</u> to build (an ark), <u>how</u> to build it (wood, tar, decks, etc.), and <u>why</u> the Lord was calling him

to build – yet he had never seen rain (faithful obedience)

- The very last verse in Genesis Chapter 6 says:
  - o "So, Noah did everything exactly as God had commanded him" *(Gen. 6:22)*
  - o This lets me know that Noah fully obeyed the radical command/ calling of God! (LHV – Lexi Howell Version)
- Some doubts Noah may have had:
  - o Whether he heard the Lord clearly
  - o What did "flood" mean?
  - o His capabilities
- Even though Noah could have possibly doubted, as anyone would, he had a relationship with God that was so strong and intimate that he knew the voice of the Lord. Noah knew that you don't have to fully understand what God is doing in order to fully obey!

♦ Obedience is hearing the voice/calling of the Lord and saying "YES!"

2. **MARY**

♦ Favored woman of God

♦ Virgin

♦ Soon to carry and give birth to the Savior of the world

♦ Like Noah, I believe that confusion, fear and doubt could have flooded Mary's mind. Yet, she only asked the angel one question *(Luke 1:34)*. If she was anything like me, she would have had many questions swirling around in her head. Nonetheless, she obeyed this radical calling of the Lord!

Look at her response:

♦ "I am the Lord's servant. May everything you have said about me come true." *(Luke 1:38)* My translation (LHV): I am the daughter of the King! Lord, do as you please!

- Mary knew who and Whose she was. But most importantly, she knew God. She trusted that whatever He said, would come to pass. For she trusted in Him.

  o Maybe like me, you wish to walk in this same wisdom and obedience of Mary. Not fully understanding the calling over your life, but fully confident in the One who called you! Oh how I wish to live out my faith in such a radical way like Mary!

Complete obedience to God requires us:

a) To know His voice for ourselves

  - The Lord speaks in many ways – through His people, from a burning bush, in the lightning, wind, through worship music, His Word, and His sweet whispers!

b) To run (*in faith*) toward the calling of your Creator

- ◆ Overcoming fear, worry, doubt and just running after the ways of the Lord!

REFLECTIVE QUESTIONS:

- ◆ How does the Lord speak to *you*?
- ◆ If you had the opportunity right now would you drop everything right where you are and run to what the Lord has called/commanded you to do? Would you surrender everything and run to your Father?

"...obedience is better than sacrifice,"

- 1 Samuel 15:22

Chapter 2

DEAR BROKEN GIRL

Come as you are, not as you should be!

Just recently, I've struggled with placing things on the throne where my ever-so loving Savior should be. I've placed a boy that I liked over the Word that gives hope. I've let Netflix consume my free time rather than giving my free time to the One who can restore my soul. I've allowed social media to be my comparison battlefield rather than letting the One who made me speak TRUE IDENTITY over me.

Do you ever just not feel *it*? You know what I mean? – "IT!" The drive or motivation to read God's Word or the feeling of His presence? It's in these moments of vulnerability that we feel worthless. Feeling overwhelmed and vulnerable happens at times, but it's what you do in those moments that determine whether or not you will soar like eagles or crash and burn. My question to you is, who do you choose to find freedom and comfort in? Is it in man or the Maker of all things, *including* man? It's such a simple question, but so many of our lives reflect the opposite of what our voices proclaim.

I mean, man it feels so good to be on the mountaintop and to truly feel and live in the presence of God! You're so on fire for Him that you honestly feel like you may explode! The feeling is so overwhelming that it never ceases to amaze me. You feel as though nothing can bring you down. You're on cloud 9 because there is a burning sensation within you to pursue your Savior relentlessly! But then, there are those moments where you wonder if the sun will ever shine again in your life. You're bombarded by all the things that the world (society) is throwing at you – work, debt, homelessness, drugs, cutting, alcohol, suicidal thoughts, pornography, hurt, heartbreak, emptiness, and the list goes on and on. You may feel as though there is this dark cloud hanging low above your head and you can't see God, not even a little bit. Heartbreak hurts. The death of a loved one is painful. Homelessness is heart-wrenching. Oh *Dear Broken Girl*, it's during these moments in life that you should draw *near* to God, not away - realizing that He sees you. He loves you and yes, He's pursuing *you*. So, when you can't feel Him or wonder why He made you go through a particular battle, remember, He's always there and His plan and provision is perfect (*Jer. 29:11*).

The past few months, I've listened to other students over Facetime, during coffee meetings or through texting, pour out their hearts to me. They've shared with me their hurts, frustrations and the feeling that they're slowly slipping from the Lord's grasp. The feeling of drifting away from the Lord's hand is a relatable topic. We must understand that we're all broken and it's okay. There will always be seasons where we have to FIGHT! Fight for what? Fight for living a life that only pleases Christ. It's during these times when we find ourselves slipping that we seek help from our brothers and sisters in Christ because that's exactly what we were made for. To encourage and motivate each other to seek Christ *first*.

"So encourage each other and build each other up..." – 1 Thessalonians 5:11

Shift your perspective

True freedom comes from continual and intentional surrendering to Christ. So whatever storm you're going through, whatever battle you're facing... **<u>IT IS WELL</u>**! Let it be well with your soul even if it is not well with your circumstances. Let the one thing that you allow to consume your day be Jesus. Dear Broken Girl, what is on the throne of your heart? Money? Work? A guy? Lust? Social media? Comparison? Self-harm? You fill in the blank!

Dear Broken Girl, how you feel does not reflect who Jesus is. We will go through seasons of tears, but only Jesus can wipe away EVERY tear. We will go through times of sorrows, but the Lord is our Comforter. We will go through times of brokenness, but only the Lord can breathe wholeness.

As I've said before, God meets us right where we are… in the midst of our brokenness. And because we are His hands, His feet, His mouthpiece, and His heartbeat, He uses us to reach those who are struggling. Through Him we are able to reassure others that they are not alone.

Drifting is easy. It takes no work to achieve it. To grow close and have an intimate relationship with the Savior, that's where the effort comes in, and it's difficult. So, what do you do when you feel like you're drifting from the One who can truly satisfy you? I don't have all the answers, but I have learned from my past battles that when I don't feel like praying, that's when I push myself *to* pray. When I feel like reading the Word is out of my reach because I'm exhausted, I dig into His Word a *bit* more. As my daddy always says, we dig, pursue, and search for the things we *truly* want.

So, when you find yourself drifting ask

yourself, "Am I drifting because I've lost intimacy with God?" or, "is the Lord taking me through a season to test my faith and loyalty to Him?" Remember our time with God is valuable. Sometimes during our drifting, God is moving things around for our benefit. It's the sweet whispers of guidance from God that keeps you going. The moment you can't hear God speaking to you, is probably because you're most likely too frantic and too busy to even settle down and listen. But hey, I get it, trust me, I do. Life has a lot happening all around us, but don't let that stop you from seeking your Savior and stretching your faith.

Maybe you're asking, "How do I do that Lexi?" Well, I think you should purposely make time for your Father. Life can get hectic at times, but if you do not set aside time to plug into the One who gives life in and of Himself *(John 4:10,14; 7: 37-39),* then you are missing out on all that God has for you.

As your friend, I also encourage you to surround yourself with people that will reassure you but will also be honest with you. That will not only pray for you but with you, comfort and encourage you. Seek accountability by telling someone who you trust and know is living for the Lord how you're feeling. A true friend will tell you the truth even if it hurts.

Things to ponder:

- ◆ It's not a "feel God's presence" thing. It's a change your perspective thing.

- ◆ In the dry seasons, remember Who has the authority to tell the rain to flow and when to stop. *(Matt. 8:26-27)*

- ◆ In the times of loneliness remember Who promises to never leave you. *(Ps. 27:10; Deut. 31:8)*

- ◆ In the moments of the unknown, remember the One Who is known for miracles, masterpieces and eternity. *(Matt. 8:2-3)*

Father,

I surrender whatever is holding me back from knowing You on a more intimate level. Father, right now I pray that You speak and that I be willing to be still, listen and obey. I love You God,

Amen.

Small moves make huge impacts

As long as you're being obedient to His Word, you are in His will. Sometimes the Lord is simply telling me to be quiet when I want to participate in a conversation, that could either please or diss Him. There is "a time to keep silent and a time to speak" *(Ecc. 3:7)*. But why would God want me to be silent when I could share some valuable information? Simple, because **the less that I hear of myself, the more I hear of Him**. He wants me to be set apart and different for His kingdom, so that others may see Christ within me. The same goes for you.

Through Him, your whole mindset, attitude, and heart is changed and renewed.

My God; my satisfaction,

You alone can satisfy the longing of my soul. My heart beats for You, whether I realize it or not. I love You!

Amen.

It's the same blood

I read a blog post that talked about the blood of Jesus and the words "*It's the same blood*" hit me like a ton of bricks. So, today, to those who feel insignificant and to those who feel superior let me remind you .... *it's the same blood.*

The blood that poured out of our Savior's body was for all of us. Only His precious blood can wash our sins white as snow (as if they never existed). *(1 John 1:7; Rev. 1:5)*. Remember Jesus doesn't pick only the prettiest, smartest or the best.

36

He sometimes chooses the weakest, the broken, and the lost. He's willing and able to cleanse us all. His death was for all. His resurrection was for all, and the veil was torn for all.

God shows no respect of persons and neither should we. If anyone feels superior over another, we must remember we are no better than the next guy. We have no reason to look down on anyone or put ourselves on a pedestal. Hear me clearly: we are *all* broken and in need of a Savior. We all have different gifts, strengths, and weaknesses, but we all serve the same Giver of gifts. Being used by God is an honor. You and I are here to serve Him, not ourselves. When you use the gifts and opportunities of God to build your own self-esteem and place it above others, you've lost focus on your true purpose. We're all born with a sinful nature...but when we dedicate our lives to Christ, our way of thinking changes. We now strive to live a selfless, Christ-centered life.

Always remember this, we are not worthy to be used by God. It is through His worthiness that we are used. Yes, our lives are valuable and have purpose. We did nothing and can never do anything to earn what He has already so freely given us. We are nothing without Him but thank God He has given us an opportunity to have an intimate and loving relationship with the Maker of the Universe. It all goes back to Jesus!

So, don't think because you're being used by God right now that it's because you did something right. No, you did nothing — He did it all. Get off your high horse and put Christ on the throne where He belongs! A faithful follower of Jesus Christ doesn't believe that they are better than anyone else. Rather, they have a firm grip on the fact they are in fact *not* better than anyone else.

We were all washed by the same blood.

You're never too far gone to come home

Have you ever messed up? Girl, same here. Too many times to count actually. Maybe you're like me and your mind has wandered a bit *too* far.

[True Life Moment #2] I was first introduced to pornography in middle school. I'm not even sure how it happened! It rapidly progressed from my thoughts to my computer or phone to my heart. I remember it consuming me to where I watched it daily in the wee hours of the morning on school nights or weekends. I lost a lot of sleep... for lust. Pornography is an addiction that is spreading like wildfire! Pornography is real! People have this misconception that pornography is only related to guys. No! Dear Broken Girl, lust attacks all ages, gender and races. After years of wrongful thinking and a lust-filled lifestyle, I can finally say that I no longer surrender to that desire, but it took Christ working in me through others to receive victory. How did I stop letting pornography consume my life?

As I grew in my faith, I knew that watching pornography and inviting wrong thoughts into my mind was not good for me [or my family] spiritually and emotionally. I constantly surrendered my wrongful thinking and actions to God, but I wasn't strong enough to stop on my own. I remember being so consumed and addicted to pornography that I was watching it right IN FRONT of my family and they didn't even know it - had no idea! How sick is that?

I remember the night that I was delivered. The worst thing ever happened — my mother caught me! Talk about a heartbreaking and heart-sinking moment. What happened Lexi? I'm glad you asked... You see one night I had told my family goodnight and that I was going to bed. Later, when I *thought* everyone was asleep, I slipped back into the family room to get my computer to take it back to my room. Unfortunately, *but* thankfully, on my way back to my room, I peeked around the corner before entering my room and looked back to see if the "coast was clear". That night.... the coast was anything but clear. There stood my mom waiting for me. You see God had revealed to my mom what was going on. She gracefully listened to the Holy Spirit and met me right where I was in the midst of my sinful state. She didn't condemn me or judge me or yell and scream at me, she simply prayed and talked to me. (We ended up talking late into the night.) Later, she made me write a letter to God apologizing and it was then I fully surrendered my pornography to Him. Pornography is an addiction and a sickness. But I'm thankful for a God who is a healer and who specializes in healing the sick and broken-hearted! That was a scary moment in my life. Through much prayer and counseling from my mom who supported and guided me to Christ to complete freedom! There was a time where it seemed like there was NO WAY out of my addiction (sickness)… but God healed me. I share this with you for several reasons. (1) To let you know that no one is perfect; (2) God has no respect of person, what He did for me and my situation, He can do the same for you; (3) God is willing and able to meet us right where we are; (4) allowing God to use you will not only be a blessing to you but could help someone else; and (5) *you're never too far gone to come back home.*

Or maybe you feel that your addiction (drugs, pornography, self-harm, gossiping, alcohol, etc.) has taken you too far for God to even see you anymore.

Dear Broken Girl, you have a Father standing with His arms stretched wide waiting for YOU. It doesn't matter what has led you astray from the promises and the fulfillment of God. Wherever you are, whatever you've done... you're never too far gone to come back home. *Luke 15:11-32.* Invite God in and let Him redeem you! Dear Broken Girl – come back home!

Father,

Thank You for reminding me that I am never too far gone to come back to You! I surrender

(_____) to You! I love You, Lord.

Amen.

Who is this Man?

The wind obeys Him! The waves cease at the whisper of His voice! Darkness is pierced in His presence *and* at the mention of His name! Again, I ask, who is this Man? A Man with such power, grace and authority. Death could not overtake Him. The grave could not hold Him. The devil couldn't trick Him. He's a man who may have been nailed to the cross, but it was His love for you and me that kept Him there! It's a love in which He desires to share with us. Maybe today you're saying, "Lexi, I'm broken, how can a Savior with so much love like that want a sinner like me?" Dear Broken Girl, I too am broken, but Jesus desires to mend our brokenness. He wants to love us until we are whole again. Maybe you're like me and you don't have an elaborate vocabulary. Girl, He doesn't care! He wants to use our limited vocabulary to speak His unlimited power and life

He wants to use our limited vocabulary to speak His unlimited power

into others. There was a time that I questioned His love and goodness for me. Why would He do this for me? This can't be right. I don't deserve to be used. I don't deserve His grace, His love, His mercy or His blessings. I am unworthy to even untie the straps of His sandals *(John 1:27)*. His whole existence is SO powerful, yet I am powerless. How can a God with such power, glory and authority want me?

Dear Broken Girl, I've messed up so many times that I've lost count… yet He still wants me, and I promise, He wants you too! Our ultimate goal is an intimate relationship with God our Father through Jesus Christ, His Son. No amount of mistakes can overcome His grace! No amount of stains can overpower His washing. God's desire for us is to live a better life and in order to fulfill that plan, He had to do one thing – send His Son to break the barrier. The barrier that sin and Satan placed between God and us. Think of it this way: when we see ourselves through the eyes of the enemy, we see ourselves as broken, unworthy, insecure, and inadequate. But when God sees us, He sees potential, beauty, worth and value with a plan to give us a better life and an opportunity to become one with Him. Maybe you're thinking, "Hold-up, hold-up, hold-up, this doesn't make sense! Somebody actually wants me just as I am? Am I *actually* worth something just as I am? *Right* where I am?" YES! YES! YES! It's difficult to comprehend; I get it. But it's true. Jesus is waiting with love and forgiveness, and honey, it's all for you.

To the one who feels lonely in a world filled with people, I've been there. Trust me, I understand. You can be in a room filled with people yet feel like you're the only one there. May I share a secret with you? It doesn't have to be that way! Jesus longs to be right by your side. He desires to talk with you, walk with you and love on you! The Bible tells us that Jesus will never leave us!

So be strong and courageous! Do not be afraid and do not panic before them. For the Lord your

God will personally go ahead of you. He will neither fail you nor abandon you."

-Deut. 31:6

Isn't it good to know that Jesus doesn't leave us when times get tough? He won't say "screw you" when your mistakes are too numerous to count. When Jesus took on the form of man, He experienced the same pain as you and I. He endured loneliness more than we would ever know. *Matthew 26* depicts a scene of Jesus experiencing loneliness. Jesus knew that His time was soon to come, so He went to pray to His Father. He also took three of His disciples with Him and told them to keep watch while He prayed. When He returned, He found them asleep. This happened THREE different times. Even though Jesus had earthly friends, He knew His true help would only come from above, from the One who knows Him fully and completely. Dear Broken Girl, you too have Someone who knows you inside and out. Well because, He made you inside and out! Jesus who knows all – knew that Judas would betray Him, yet He never said a word, never called him out, shut him out or cast him aside, never betrayed him, or gossiped to the others about him – Jesus simply loved him! WOW! Just let that wash over you. *That's* the God we serve!

"You shaped me first inside, then out; you formed me in my mother's womb. I thank you, High God - you're breathtaking! Body and soul, I am marvelously made! I worship in adoration - what a creation!" - Psalm 139: 13-14

Who better to know us than the One who created us? You may be thinking, "You don't understand Lexi, my mistakes are numerous!" I am guilty of this also. But, trust me when I say, it's okay! He doesn't hold it against you, in fact, He has wiped our slate clean, but first you have to become one with

Him in order to receive the cleanliness He brings.

Let me assure you, you are not in your brokenness alone. Don't single yourself out! Don't look down on yourself! You are beneath no one! His whole existence was to break the barrier, release the chains (sin), that the world through Satan has bound you with. His grace is freely given. Meaning you don't have to *earn* what is *freely* given.

Dear Broken Girl, your mistakes don't define you. Sin no longer has to be your master! You have an opportunity to be free! This freedom comes through Jesus Christ. I have read, heard and experienced the glory of the Lord. Trust me, this is definitely something you want to experience! My life has been changed, and my chains have been broken, piece by piece! Again, you, too, can experience the freedom that only Jesus brings.

Sin no longer has to be your master

For the longest, I felt that I had no purpose, worth or value, and I'm not going to lie, it still creeps into my mind at times. You may be feeling the same way. However, it doesn't have to be like this! Jesus died because He saw potential in us. He instilled a purpose in which only He can fulfill in each one of us. Christ wants us! Christ loves us! Christ died for us! Christ ROSE for us! We are His masterpiece! You don't have to be perfect to be used! You don't have to look like a model to be used. You don't have to be a size zero for Him to think that you're beautiful. You don't have to be the smartest for Him to feel that you are worth something. He wants you to be His, just as you are, flaws and all. Be real. Be yourself. He just wants you to want Him. Don't you see? God looks at you and sees His wonderfully made creation. Every time God sees you, He is blown away by your beauty! *Dear Broken Girl*, God is so in love with *you*! He smiles

He is overjoyed because now your heart beats with His

at every moment you give Him His breath back through worship and prayer. He looks at you and when He sees you, girl, He is overjoyed because now your heart beats with His. He doesn't look at your fancy clothes or makeup. No, He looks at the *real* you – the you beyond your outer appearance. In *1 Samuel 16:7*, the Lord tells Samuel, *"Do not judge by his appearance or height, for I have rejected him. The Lord doesn't see things the way we see them. People judge by outward appearance, but the Lord looks at the heart."* To some that may seem scary because you don't like who you really are on the outside or inside. So, I encourage you to change your attitude, to change the way you treat others and yourself. Can we just strip Satan of his lies in a moment? No, it's not an overnight change, but it's a dedicated to Christ change. Dear Broken Girl, just in case no one has told you today, let me be the first to say that you are so beautiful, adored, cherished and loved. Being comfortable and confident in *your* skin is where we *all* need to be.

He's a good, good Father

I can see it now: Jesus physically wiping away all those things by which we define ourselves. I can see Him using His blood (makeup remover) washing away the mascara, the foundation, and setting spray. He's wiping away one by one our insecurities of not being "good enough". Each stain, blemish and sin is being washed away by the blood of Jesus. He brushes our hair taking out the highlights, bleach, extensions and with each stroke, He reveals His truth in us, about us and around us. With each stroke, Jesus counts the strand and says, *"You're chosen", "I love you", "Remember this forever and always, it was I who bore the cross for you, not the world", "You're beautiful and most importantly, you are My child!"*

The Lord delights in who you truly are, not who you pretend to be. He looks at you "fresh-faced" and rejoices at His creation! Why? Because He made you in His own image and He makes no mistakes.

Then God said, "Let Us make human beings in our image, to be like Us ..."

-Genesis 1:26

Broken to Broken

Broken: having given up all hope; despairing.

I'm inspired when I see *broken* people come to the realization and experience the truth that being *broken* is okay. The state of not being "okay" *is* okay. Life happens. Pain is inflicted. Death occurs. Mistakes are made. However, the truth behind it all is that you're not alone. Jesus died so that we may live again! We are no longer in this battle alone, but rather we have Someone fighting the battle along with us. And guess what y'all? I've read the end of The Book... and in the end Jesus wins! Even when we can't see it. Even in the unknown, the valleys and the darkness; He is there! Our brokenness is an opportunity for God to step in, show a little muscle and provide His wholeness. Jesus is known as the Prince of Peace (Jehovah Shalom). Peace meaning wholeness. In our brokenness, He is whole. In fact, His strength works best in our weaknesses. So, today if nothing is going as planned... if everything seems like it's falling apart... if life seems to be slapping you in the face, *Dear Broken Girl*, **IT IS WELL!** If it is not well with your circumstances, let it be well with your soul. Remember His truths about you and the promises He has spoken over you.

He knows the plans He has for you *(Jer. 29:11)*. He died so that you may inherit a life more abundantly than the one you are currently living *(John 10:10)*. He knows the number of hairs on your head *(Luke 12:7)*. He created the galaxy, yet He still knows you individually and personally and He understands your struggles. He has *your* name written in His book *(Luke 10:20b)*. Your life is all planned out by Him! Now, rest in Him.

I have a friend who works best in our brokenness
and His name is Jesus!

So, from one broken girl to another, you are
not alone. Your brokenness may make you feel this
way but know these three things: (1) God is with you;
(2) I am praying for you and (3) together through
Christ we can overcome 'this'! Whatever your "this"
is! **Nothing** is too big for our God!

Father,
I know that I am broken, but that is okay
because in my brokenness You are there. And let
that promise alone be well with my soul. I love
You.
Amen.

Falling at the feet of Jesus

There's something so special about the feet of Jesus! Time and time again we hear stories in the Bible involving the feet of our forever faithful King.

When you get a chance read:

- **Luke 7:37-38**: a story of a *sinful* woman washing the feet of Jesus with her tears, wiping it with her hair, kissing His feet.
- **Mark 5:22**: A synagogue leader by the name of Jairus, falls at the feet of Jesus begging Him to heal his sick daughter.
- **Mark 5:33**: describes a woman bleeding internally who falls at Jesus' feet and touches the cloak of His garment, and receives Jesus' healing.
- **John 1:27**: is about John the Baptist who states that he isn't even worthy to untie the straps on Jesus' feet!

♦ **<u>Luke 8:28</u>**: tells us how demons bow at His feet at the mention of His name and in His presence

All these people were broken in some way. They needed healing, a blessing, a way out! They humbled themselves to the only One who has the authority to tell the wind to cease and the wind obeys! The One who has the power to bring a dead man back to life. His name is JESUS! He is the way, the truth and the light!

We hear countless times that we should lay our worries, our burdens and our lives at the feet of Jesus, at the foot of the cross. Why? It's an act of submission/worship - an opportunity to proclaim, "Savior, I am less, but You are more!" We bow in reverence of who He is. We must understand that we are nothing without Jesus. The feet we bow down to were pierced for us! Oh HALLELUJAH for a King who does not send us away, but rather embraces us and whispers in our ear, "My love, stay".

Imagine a broken girl crouched down in her room crying out to God! She doesn't understand what's going on. Why is death and darkness overtaking her family? Why is she constantly suffering? She cries out to Him! No words can form, just tears flow. The weight of the world is beginning to overwhelm her. She has a calling over her life to be different, to use her life as a vessel to bring His name glory, but she's hurting right now! She's pouring out her heart to God asking Him for a sign, a message, something... ANYTHING! I can see Jesus hanging on the cross whispering, "My child, get up..." He looks at her through His swollen, bloodstained eyes *and He sees her*. She's reminded that the pain He experienced then is to take away the pain she is experiencing now. *Dear Broken Girl*, He sees you! He understands you, but most importantly He's here for you. You are not alone.

How many times have we said, "God, this is not something that I say lightly, but if being wounded leads me to know more of You, well then, Lord, I'm ready. I'm ready to know You, glorify You and to build Your kingdom"? It's when times get tough that most people pull out their dusty Bibles or download a Bible app or pray to God like never before. It's like they now understand that they can't handle this situation on their own, so they relinquish all power, authority and control to the One who can truly handle their mess and turn it into a message. It's in the dark, lonely, wounded times we lean in closer to a Higher power. Don't discredit or become discouraged or wish away your pain. There is a purpose within it, a plan for it and a God whose presence over shines our weaknesses. Take heart, for Jesus has overcome the world! *(John 16:33)*

Dear Broken Girl... it's time to fight back!

No longer should you *allow* fear to control you. You were never made to succumb to fear. You were made to fight fear with faith! Your friends shouldn't control you - your insecurities shouldn't define you. You are made to truly be free! *(John 8:36)* You are a warrior. A fighter. A survivor. Lies were spread about you because you have the Spirit of Truth living within you. It's time to fight back! Now, I'm not talking about physical fighting - No, I'm speaking about the freedom and the faith that Jesus alone can bring. Your 'crush' was not made to control and consume your whole day. Your whole day should succumb to the Father and His glory. Don't let the task overwhelm you to the point of frustration, rather, defeat it with the heart of a servant. So, Dear Broken Girl, FIGHT! For there is a war raging. Put on the whole armor of God. What is the armor of God? I'm glad you asked.

Stand firm then, with the **belt of truth** buckled around your waist, with the **breastplate of righteousness** in place, and with your feet fitted with the readiness that comes from the **gospel of peace.** In addition to all this, take up the **shield of faith**, with which you can extinguish all the flaming arrows of the evil one. Take the **helmet of salvation** and the **sword of the Spirit,** which is the word of God. And **pray** in the Spirit on all occasions with all kinds of prayers and requests." - **Ephesians 6:14-18**

With this in mind, be alert, stand firm and remember to continuously pray for one another. Do you have on your armor? Not anyone else's armor, but *YOUR* armor, the one specifically made for you. You are not made to be defeated; you are an overcomer! Don't let sin overwhelm you or the lies of Satan bombard you! Fight back! For you are a warrior.

My God; my Warrior,

Give me the supernatural strength to fight back!
Your Word says that Your children are not fighting
against flesh and blood (humans) but against spirits
(within them). Now, let Your Spirit overpower all
other spirits that may come against me! Remind me
that I'm not made to bow down in fear, but to stand
firm in faith! I love You.

Amen.

Chapter 3

I'D RATHER BE SINGLE

Until Jesus becomes the reason you live, your

life has not truly begun

I love compliments. Hearing those sweet words about *me* just does something to my heart. It makes me feel special, important and loved. I mean let's be honest, don't we all wish to feel this way? Whether you want to admit it or not, most of us do. One of my hang-ups are sappy, romantic love stories! I love them! The love-hate types are my all-time favorite. We've all seen it, the girl hates the guy or isn't interested or plays hard to get, but the guy is so in-love with her that he continues to pursue her. He believes that she is worth the pursuit. And although she rejects him repeatedly, it's okay, because to him, she is worth it all. The rejection doesn't stop him, and the time apart from her doesn't lessen his feelings for her. He is relentless in his pursuit of her because she means just that much to him. Guess what? Our sweet, heavenly Father pursues us the same way! A relentless, fearless and never-ending pursuit. Although romantic movies make me happy, they always find a way to make me feel empty. However, with Jesus, I am never empty. Rather *in* Him I find my fulfillment and satisfaction. When I'm watching a movie, I tend to place myself into their story and dream that I'm the girl that this handsome man is fighting for, loves and adores. Sadly, reality hits me when *"The End"* rolls across my screen. The storyline that I fantasized about is not my story. It's make-believe (fiction), it's Hollywood. One of my deepest desires is to experience true love. Love that consists more than picnic dates, holding hands and the occasional "I love you" sentiments. But you know what, the Lord is writing *my* story and it begins and ends with Him. Therefore, I will wait on the Lord and trust that in due time my prince will come.

Have you ever noticed that the Lord uses our lowest moments for His greatest impact and blessing? I had always believed that I was single because I wasn't "pretty enough". The devil would constantly place these thoughts in my mind. He truly had me fooled and even though I recognize his lies; I find myself still believing them at times. But what does 'being pretty' or 'pretty enough' even mean?

Why is there a certain way that I must look, a certain weight that I must weigh to be considered beautiful? Dear Broken Girl, society will tell you that the reason you're single is because you don't fit in "this" box. A box designed by society. May I share something with you? You're beautiful, how do I know? Because God says so! How many times do you ride down the road and look up at the sky and say "wow – beautiful!"? Well, honey, the same Creator of those beautiful skies is the same Creator of you and me. He took His time molding us just the way He pictured us –perfect in His sight. His desire is for each of us to be different - unique even. For you were not born to fit in - no ma'am; you were born to stand out! The animals on this earth are incredible, the skies are painted beautifully, but you and I, we are His masterpieces! You, Dear Broken Girl, are a masterpiece! His pride and joy!

Or maybe people say you're single because you're "too Christian". Ever heard of that? Yeah, me too. I've heard that many times and it's so NOT

TRUE! We are mature girls in our faith! In other words, we are women of faith who refuse to settle for anything less than God's best for us! You've matured spiritually to understand that your life is valuable to God and should not be freely given to just anyone. We've heard the lies that, "Maybe if you weren't so uptight and learned how to 'live a little', then you would have a boyfriend and have some fun!" Sounds tempting, doesn't it? Not really. Understand that you can live a life of fun without sacrificing and suppressing your faith.

Singleness is not a time to trudge through, but rather, to grow through. The world will say you're nothing, but Jesus will remind you that in Him, you are everything! Be encouraged today and know that singleness is a sacred season, embrace it!

Temptation

For as long as I can remember I have always wanted to be liked by everyone. Going from preschool to high school I wanted to be surrounded by friends constantly. During my middle school years, I began to see things (life, friends, and this world) differently. It was during my seventh-grade year that I invited my precious Savior into my life. My family surrounded me in prayer, and I began to hear the veil tear in my life. From that day on, I was changed. My eyes were opened. My new life, my *true* life, had now begun. Living for Christ changes EVERYTHING! Not only did it begin to transform how I talked, walked and lived in the coming years; it also showed me that being single is not as bad as people proclaim it to be.

My relationship was not in the realm of God and therefore was toxic

Remember this – temptation is real… always waiting for us to take the first bite. The beginning of my junior year, I met a guy. This was my first serious relationship and I had no idea what I was doing! I had not truly learned, nor did I believe that a guy could not satisfy what I was deeply longing for – COMPANIONSHIP! But you see, what I deeply longed for could only be filled by my Savior. The Word of God tells us that we should not match up with someone who is not seeking the same thing (or the same Someone - Jesus). We call that being unequally-yoked *(2 Corinthians 6:14)*. My relationship was not in the realm of God and therefore was toxic. My desire was to seek and serve God, his was not. We had differences that would always rub me the wrong way, yet still I remained in the relationship. I'm sure you're wondering why? Well, it's because I chose to ignore who I was or more importantly, Whose I was (God's). I thought being in an earthly relationship would make me happy. I believed the lies that I was only beautiful, only had worth because some guy took an interest in me. Boy, was I wrong! He wasn't a Christian or at least he didn't follow the lifestyle of Christ and he didn't "mind" that I was. It didn't bother him that I was a Christian, but it did bother me that he wasn't. I ignored those feelings. He had struggles! Struggles in which I couldn't help him with because I had my own struggles that I was trying to overcome. He was surrounded by drugs and unfortunately, he was also using. Several times I pleaded with him to stop and attempted to speak identity over him. But, how could I speak life and identity over someone else without knowing or fully understanding the identity that has been spoken over me? Throughout that brief relationship, the Lord kept telling me to 'let it go'. To let him go. To let the lies go. I fought with the Lord constantly over ending this relationship. Finally, it took an 'involuntarily' chat with my mom who was informed by God (a vision) about some out of character things going on in my life. Things that were not in the will of God. I eventually ended the relationship and surrendered in desperation to know Jesus more. At first, it was difficult, but I began to see this guy's true colors. My eyes were no longer blinded by the lies but opened by the truth through Jesus. I've made mistakes, fought God and failed in many ways, but I do not regret that time in my life. Why? Because fully surrendering it all to God is where my faith truly began. Fast forward a few months later and I found myself constantly in the Word learning about who the Lord says that I am in Him and who He is in me. I am His daughter, His bride, His friend, His servant, His princess. He's my real first love, my King, my Savior, my Best Friend, my Father, my Healer, and my Lover until the end of time.

Total surrender to God

Who knew that I would begin to see the healing hand of God work so graciously in my life in the next few moments. It all started in February 2018, my

mema became extremely ill *(I'll discuss this more in a later chapter)*. During those dark days, I often wished I had a boyfriend to hold me, to comfort me and tell me that it was going to be okay, that my mema was going to be okay. I **needed** a boyfriend to love me through the pain because during those moments I was beyond broken. But when I look back now at that time, *I was being held* by Jesus Himself. He wiped my tears away. Jesus showed me that *man cannot do what a Maker is destined for.* I was a single, broken teen, but thank God for His Son who works best in my brokenness. *("My grace is sufficient for you, for my power is made perfect in weakness."- 2 Cor. 12:9)*

Will I be single forever God?

I know the subtitle of this chapter ("Will I be single forever God?") contradicts almost everything that I've talked about so far but let's be real, most of us have posed this question to God at one time or another. Am I right? We've all wondered about the day we will meet that "special" someone! The guy you've been praying for, dreaming about and longing to see! It's okay to want a man to share life with. *CAUTION*: If you're looking for a guy, make sure that his faith lines up with yours. In other words, pray to God for a Christ-filled man, someone that He has specifically designed for you. Someone whose life lines up with the Word, **not** the world. The same applies to you. We shouldn't expect something from someone that we're not willing to allow for ourselves. Ladies, you have a responsibility in your season of singleness and that is to let the Lord use your life to bring His Name glory and your heart joy.

Not everyone that looks or breathes your way is worth your breath. Not every guy that gives you the time of day is worth your time. Many ladies have had their purpose and focus all misconstrued. They are meeting guys on Saturday and by Sunday they've already given him the opportunity to take control of their lives. If you fall into this category answer this question (be honest) – Are you possibly settling for the "anything" because you're afraid to be alone? FOMO = fear of missing out. Such an awful feeling to have, but a common one to say the least. Listen to me, the devil knows what great plans God has for each of us, therefore he desires to distract us. There's a nation FULL of people that he will use to redirect and/or pause your purpose. Wake up already! Loneliness is real… it is, but *Dear Broken Girl,* so is God. SO IS GOD! In our weakness and loneliness, I encourage you to surround yourself with other Christian sisters. We are to remember that we were made for *community*. What is community? It involves surrounding ourselves with people of faith. People that will uplift us, encourage us, support us, and pray for us. Community is key in our faith journey and in our everyday lifestyle. Today, I feel that we have lost sight on the sweetest thing the Lord has given us – each other.

When most people hear the word 'singleness' they instantly associate it with loneliness, and while at times that may be true, singleness is so much more than that. I used to (and still do at times) constantly feed my mind with romantic comedy movies and I constantly fantasized about how, who and where I would meet my future husband. I would picture how he would look physically, but also act spiritually. I've even prepared how I want my wedding to be on a Pinterest board. I'm telling you guys, when it comes to me, I love the thought of meeting the man that the Lord has designed *specifically for me* and just letting my mind wander on the things that I hope we can do together – such as travel, raise a family, etc. Trust me when I say this - this is not healthy. I've had to submit this to God constantly. It's through much prayer and submission to the Holy Spirit that my desire to meet my husband has become less and less. I believe that in order to be completely satisfied in my singleness, I need to be *fully* focused on who God wants me to be and what He wants me to do. After all, I am His daughter, and, as always, *Papa knows best.* During my season of waiting though, I'm praying that the Lord is molding my future husband. I never want to rush the hand of God. In my season of singleness, I can grow physically, emotionally, mentally, and of course spiritually. I hope that in my waiting I can fulfill the plans the Lord has for my life at this moment, not wondering or being bound by the feelings of my future. I realize that in order for me to be the absolute best friend/girlfriend it requires me to become the best daughter to my Savior first. *Dear Broken Girl,* the road will not be easy, but will it be worth it? ABSOLUTELY!

Have you ever thought about that maybe Jesus is pruning you to become what your future boyfriend is praying for you to be? It takes time. It takes growth. It takes Jesus. Perhaps he's praying for a sweet, compassionate and loving girlfriend. In order for that to be accomplished, you must let the Lord fulfill His work within you *first.* And it doesn't happen instantly, but it must be woven into your being.

Who You Are

You are... His bride, His child, His princess. You are a servant of the Most High God. You are fearless, a person of power. You are loved. You are His church, a leader through Christ, an encourager for Christ. You were made to relate to others. You are vital to the lives of others, to meet people right where they are, you are set apart, loved, chosen, pursued, fearfully and wonderfully made. You are Christ's heartbeat, His mouthpiece, His hands, and His feet. You were made in His image. You are unique. You are treasured. Your life has been spoken for and over. You are beautiful, accepted, and forgiven. You are His beloved. Through the eyes of Christ, you were worth dying for. You were bought at a very high price. You are wanted... adored. You are His first love!

Set boundaries

A lot of times we're SO READY for a relationship that we forfeit or forget to set boundaries. Maybe you pledge not to have sex until marriage, or perhaps you told your boyfriend that you wanted to wait until marriage, and he responded that he doesn't mind waiting. It's great to say you are setting boundaries, but it's another thing to *actually* set them and stand by them.

One of my love languages is physical touch; therefore, I have to be careful where I allow a guy to touch me even if his intentions are innocent. Most of us know that touching can lead us to a place we're not ready to go. Another problem for me is when my boyfriend becomes my sole focus rather than Christ. It's then that I must step back, readjust and refocus on Christ. Your boyfriend is to be your companion, not your god. He is to be someone you share life with not someone who takes hostage or consumes your life because it revolves solely around him. Realizing and setting boundaries whether physical, spiritual or emotional ensures that the guy you are interested in will not jeopardize your walk with Christ.

In my singleness, I have found that it's important for me to set boundaries for my heart to beat with God's. What do I mean by that? Well, I so easily lose focus on my worth by placing my value in how many guys look my way or pursue me. So, I have to constantly remind myself, "Lexi, you are made for more. They cannot satisfy you like Jesus can. Remember Whose you are." Does this work? It takes time and practice, but yes it works for me. My question for you today is, what boundaries do you need to set in your relationship and/or everyday life? Remember, be honest with yourself because we can't fool God. He is all-knowing (Omniscience). God already knows the truth, but your transparency (honesty) is what He delights in.

Your transparency (honesty) is what He delights in

If you're not really sure about what boundaries to set, I encourage you to simply ask God. Yes, it's really that simple.

"Father,

Reveal to me any boundaries You desire for me to place in my life whether personal or romantic.

Lord, help me to remember who I am in my single, dating, and married years -- Yours. You are the God who never fails me and continues to love me. Thank You! I love You!

Amen."

Promise Ring

My daddy and I had a date night one night. (this
was after my boy incident) I had just turned 17.
We had dinner at Simple Twist in Smithfield, NC.
(Simple cheeseburger with fries – mmm!).
Anyway, he and I talked and then when our meal
was over, he presented me with my promise ring.
And I made a promise to my daddy and God that
I would wait until marriage.

Love you daddy! <3

Don't date just to pass the time

How many people have dated, had sex and jumped from relationship to relationship to simply "pass time"? Nothing is permanent to them. Everything seems temporary – and to a certain extent, this is true.

Dear Broken Girl, if you are dating just to pass the time, then you are planting a seed of brokenness, hatred and betrayal. A brokenness that comes from believing the lies of the enemy. Lies that you can find fulfilment from casual sex or dating. Lies that the more compliments you receive determines your beauty or your worth.

Even when you don't choose Him first, you will always be first to Him

The compliments will fade. The boys will fail in their promises. But God? He will NEVER fail you! His love, existence and presence are never-ending. He is Omnipresent. True satisfaction is found in Him.

This world will fade, but He will always remain. He is the beginning and the end. *(John 22:13, Heb. 12:2)* He promises that He will never fail you like people do. Why? Because He loves you way too much. So much that He gave His only Son for you and I *(John 3:16)*. Even when you don't choose Him first, you will always be first to Him.

Dear Broken Girl, you are so beautiful! Let your beauty deep within your soul shine so bright that it overflows to the outside. You should exude confidence because your confidence is found in Jesus, not in yourself, and definitely not in someone else.

> Don't be concerned about the outward beauty of fancy hairstyles, expensive jewelry, or beautiful clothes. You should clothe yourselves instead with the beauty that comes from within, the unfading beauty of a gentle and quiet spirit, which is so precious to God.
>
> -1 Peter 3:3-4

Have you ever deliberately chosen something over Jesus? Sleep? A guy? Food? ...Guilty! I have chosen all of those things and more over my faithful God. I've told God, "Five more minutes and then I'm Yours!" Twenty minutes later and I still haven't given God the time He so well deserves. It's awful! So why do I constantly make the same mistakes? Flesh! The Bible tells us that the Spirit within us is willing to do right, but the flesh is weak. *(Matthew 26:41)*

The devil uses our laziness to distance us from God. Listen, we're human and we screw up, but it's okay because I know a God who specializes and works best in our weaknesses *(2 Cor. 12:9)*. Despite my shortcomings, the Lord has shown Himself faithful time and time again.

Maybe today you're frustrated with the fact that you've chosen 'created' things over the Creator. You're not alone! Dear Broken Girl, we all fall short. We're all guilty of placing created things before our Creator. The good news is that our Creator is willing to forgive us and give us a second chance. How? Simply surrendering the desire or weakness to God and allowing Him to work in your heart. There's so much beauty and freedom in you! Be content in your life, your skin, your God.

"....for I have learned to be content whatever the circumstances". - Philippians 4:11

Maybe others have turned the page to a new chapter in their lives; dating, engagement, college, jobs and you haven't yet. Hear me clearly - it's okay! You have so much to bring to this world. It takes time to fully experience the joy that the Lord longs to give you. Because I become so easily consumed with a guy rather than God, I know that having a guy right now would distract me from fully embracing all that God has for me to do for Him. Maybe you have this same mindset and that's why the Lord is whispering to you, "Not right now." Or maybe it's for a different reason. Pray about it. Don't dwell on it; just live in the freedom that singleness and Jesus brings.

What are you connected to?

(Or better yet *who* are you connected to?)

When your phone is connected to Wi-Fi and you're able to go on social media or send an email, everything is great. Maybe your connections are really strong at home or at a local coffee shop. Wherever you find it, however you find it, you're happy (content). We live in a world that not only revolves around us but in a world where we revolve *around* our electronic devices. Personal interaction (social media), business interaction, tutoring sessions and job applications all happen electronically. If we try to access social media but our Wi-Fi is weak or out of range, it sends us in a panic mode. I mean let's be honest, most of us would be lost without our electronic devices.

One day, while I was riding by a McDonald's restaurant, on the side of the window I saw, "**FREE WI-FI**" posted in big, bold letters. Why is it so important that a restaurant or any company would draw so much attention to the fact that they have free Wi-Fi? Because they know this will get our attention, offering us what we *so desperately "need"* – WI-FI (our lifeline). And in return, they get what they want (our money). The stronger the Wi-Fi, the better. Why? Because the stronger the signal, the more we are able to connect in a faster timeframe. We're able to complete our tasks and so much more. We don't want something weak because if the Wi-Fi is too slow, then our patience begins to decrease and frustration, anxiety and our temper begins to increase. Weak Wi-Fi is looked down upon and only used when there seems to be no other option of a stronger connection.

How many of us use this logic when it comes to our lives? We're constantly seeking people to surround us who can validate us. People who provide us with a *strong* relationship/friendship. Someone who provides us with joy, peace, love and stability. But a lot of times our actions in finding friends is like us choosing weak Wi-Fi; we settle for what we can get because it's better than having nothing at all. In other words, this was the "best we could find". Have you ever noticed that your "weak Wi-Fi" consists mostly of all the things found ***outside*** of the will of God? He alone is your strong, dependable, always available "Wi-Fi". If you would just plug into Him, you will then have access to everything you need, want or desire. Blessings, hope, guidance and breakthroughs that the weak sources could never supply. How easy we mix up what is strong, substantial and everlasting for something weak, wavering and "the best we could find."

I encourage you to exam your heart and your "sources" because what you connect to will show how you value yourself and who you are within. Connecting with people that know of Jesus but not living for Him or worst yet those who don't know Jesus at all, will keep you in a broken cycle connected to weak Wi-Fi leaving you frustrated, confused, lost and empty. Connect with God, the Creator of ALL things! Don't get me wrong; connecting to Christ does not mean you will not face brokenness, lost friendships, backbiting, gossiping, betrayal, and the list goes on. You will also experience battles, some you will win and some you will lose but when you realize *Who* you're connected to, it makes the battles seem a bit more worthwhile.

Father,
Thank You for being my strong, dependable source of Wi-Fi. In You, every good thing follows. Help me to plug into You and You alone. I love You.
Amen.

A Date with My Heavenly Father!

I spoke earlier in the book about going on a date with my dad. But let me tell you something that is much more rewarding and that is having a date with my heavenly Father. A good way to learn the real you is to date the One who created you! Sounds like a weird concept, right? But really, it's freeing! When you begin to date God, you surrender yourself to Him and by doing this, you begin to learn to love you. You begin to discover the One Who made you and His purpose for you. So, I encourage you to go on dates with Him (dinner, movies, shopping). I won't lie, at first going on dates with God is a bit intimidating because it's out of our norm, but it really is freeing! Treat your date with God like you would any other individual. Make plans! Dress up! Pamper yourself!

Just like many other women, I love the idea of cuddling, snuggling, picnic dates, late night strolls, back of the truck movies under the stars, simply grabbing a bite to eat at the in-&-out burger joint. The thought of some of these things just makes my heart melt! These things are great, but what I find much more satisfying are the conversations I have with my Father. He is so strong, and confident but not arrogant. Knowledgeable but not conceited. Loving but not overbearing. He's a great listener and guidance counselor but never negative or condescending. He is such a beautiful person and He made a beautiful masterpiece – you and me. Not only did He form us *(Jer. 1:5; Ps. 139:13)*, He desires to pursue, love and grow us to where we can experience a better life, not only in this life, but the next life to come (Eternity). My conversations with God are never sugarcoated like the ones that I may have with a co-worker, friend, significant other or parent. No, they are real and vulnerable conversation. What would it benefit for me to lie to the One who knows all – even my thoughts?

Have you ever gone through a 'life' situation, and felt all alone, like you had no one to talk to?

Well, guess what? You're wrong! Our Heavenly Father is the best Person to turn to. He's always there, always listening, always caring. You have a Father who desires to have a relationship with you. *Talk to Him*. Write to Him. Sing to Him. It doesn't have to be an elaborate, well thought out conversation or speech that you have researched and perfected. One of the many good things about our Father is that you can be real with Him. You do not have to worry about your vocabulary. It's okay if our verbs, adjectives and nouns don't mix. He simply wants to hear from you, to have an intimate relationship with you.

Dear Broken Girl, how great is it to know that you have access to the best Father, Friend, Counselor, Listener in the whole wide world? Yes, you may have friends that tell you, "If you ever need me, no matter the time of day, I am here for you." And they may very well mean it and they may have great intentions, but sometimes tiredness, emotions, and life can get in the way. Thankfully, we serve a

God who is always available to us! He has the one and only true 24/7 hotline. And not just any hotline, but an everlasting one!

Boyfriend wanted – not needed

I am taking this season of singleness and being intentional in it. Having a guy friend is great! I won't lie, one of my future desires is to have a Christian boyfriend, then eventually marriage, and a family of my own; *but* I don't want to miss out on the here and now. Right here and right now is the time for me to form an intimate relationship with God. A time to get to know myself in Him. A time to learn what He desires for me. A time to learn His voice from that of the enemy. I know, I know, the title of this chapter is *I'd Rather Be Single* and that's true, but that doesn't mean that I don't want a Christian companion. I believe it's important that I pray for and over my future, this includes boyfriend/husband. This is something that I do daily because when the time comes, God is going to give me the desires of my heart by blessing me with the man He has molded for me. I also have chosen to write to my future 'him' about some of my life journeys (I'll explain more in a later chapter).

So, maybe you don't have that special someone at this age in your life, so what? Perhaps there is a reason for that and maybe that reason is that you simply need to spend time with God to figure out - well... YOU! Please hear me when I say this, there is nothing wrong with dreaming, believing, hoping and praying for that special someone, but we have to be careful, we have to let God have control over it. This means that we can't get caught up in the 'dream' and allow it to control our lives *(Phil. 4:8)*. In other words, you can't let the fantasy life determine your real life. We have to maintain control of the battles that's always going on within our minds. This is how the devil traps us. He consumes our minds. One thing I've learned is that the devil is not just after your dreams, your health or your mind.

He's after your JOY!! The Bible tells us that the joy of the Lord is our strength *(Neh. 8:10)*. Girls, we can't let our dreams override our reality. I encourage you to seek God and allow His will to be your will. His desires to be your desires. *(Ps. 37:4)*

Answer this: If you had that one *'thing'* that you have dreamed of all your life **right now**, would your focus shift from the Creator to the created thing or remain on the Creator? In all honesty, there are times when I would put God on the backburner and put all my focus on that one *'thing'* I most wanted. Here's the deal, anything that God has designed for us to have will not distract us from who He is, but it will motivate us to know more of Him. Anything that God is the center of will not cause confusion, but it will bring light and clarification.

Chapter 4

YEAH, ME TOO

Broken pieces make beautiful
masterpieces in the end

The freedom only He brings

Ever had a part of your body that you didn't like (thighs, nose, eyebrows, etc.)? Yeah, me too. I personally believe that to "love yourself" is to be confident in who you are *right* where you are! That, Dear Broken Girl, is the true definition of freedom found in Christ. When you find freedom in Christ, you no longer believe the lies of the devil because you have the truth of the Bible written on your heart. Your worth is not defined by the opinion of others; so stop giving their opinions power over you. There is something bigger than our mistakes and frustrations. Seek that Source. Seek the Source that says that you're worth it no matter what. Seek the Cross!

Remember that your identity is NOT in what others think of you, and your value is not determined by what others say about you.

I love it when people think they have something on you and call out your past mistakes. They bring it up like it still has a hold on you; like it's going to embarrass you or send you on a rampage. It's funny because they don't know what you know or better yet they don't know Who you know. They don't know that your past has been forgiven and forgotten by the only One who truly matters. They don't know that your past is just that - your past. They don't know that you can now smile about what once had you bound/captive because you have now been set free. Your chains have been broken! That particular sin, mistake or battle is no longer yours, but the Lord's. So, yes, I openly share my weaknesses and shortcomings for I know Who holds my future.

So, call me out about a past relationship or a judgment I made or gossip that I partook in, because now I've given that burden to Someone greater than you and me. He does not judge... He loves. He bore the cross for me, which included my  mistakes and yes, yours too. So, when people come at you bringing back things that you've already laid down at the feet of Jesus, stand firm in the fact that you have been delivered. Dear Broken Girl, the enemy will use whatever or whomever he wants in order to tear us down, but we've been built on a more solid foundation and we are rooted and grounded in Someone so much greater, a foundation in which no man, not even the devil or his demons can tear down.

You know, it's funny how God works. He takes something that once had you bound and held captive and He uses that same something to not only free you but someone else as well. I talked earlier about my past relationship, even though it was toxic, so many things, good and bad, have sprung from this relationship. I went through a dark time. A time where my family began to see the darkness surrounding this relationship overshadowing the light of God within me. During this short timeframe, I was stressed, broken, and hurt. I had a deep desire to feel loved and pursued. Unfortunately, I sought that satisfaction in a guy who was not designed to fulfill what I desperately longed for. I often heard that when God allows us to go through challenges, that it's not only for us but for someone else too. Well, let me tell you, it's true. Several months later I have been given the opportunity to help teens through confusion, heartbreak and emotional toxic relationships with Christ as my guide. Christ knew that my brokenness would lead to someone else's breakthrough and become a testament of just how good and forgiving God is.

Money, Money, Money!

"But people who long to be rich fall into temptation and are trapped by many foolish and harmful desires that plunge them into ruin and destruction. For the love of money is the root of all kinds of evil. And some people, craving money, have wandered from the true faith and pierced themselves with many sorrows"

- 1 Timothy 6:9-10

THE WAS ME! Better yet, this is still me! My parents constantly tell me and others that I don't care about money (bank account, cash, how much something costs). I totally agree that this was me in a nutshell, or so I thought. But these two verses called me out and showed me my true colors. Like most teens, I desire to buy and have new trending clothing.

I live my life off of Pinterest. It's so bad that before I can try on an outfit, I have to look it up online to see how other people put similar outfits together! Pathetic, right? My mom is constantly encouraging me to put my own trend together. I guess you could say that I'm addicted to Pinterest. I actually find a sense of joy from looking at all the outfits I wish I had. I can spend hours upon hours on Pinterest – just surfing. No big deal, right? WRONG! Remember I said earlier that daydreaming is one of my biggest setbacks. I can spend hours upon hours on Pinterest just wishing for things that I nor my parents can afford; hours upon hours wishing that my skin was as smooth as 'her' skin; my hair was naturally curly like 'hers'; my shape was shaped like 'her' shape and the list goes on and on. This eventually became my downfall. You see, I was constantly comparing myself to the world, I was in a sense telling God that I was not pleased with His workmanship of me. That He got it wrong… even worst, He made some mistakes when He designed me. Comparison is so destructive, yet we so easily succumb to it.

Dear Broken Girl, happiness is found from within. Happiness is about being content right where we are, with what we have and how we look. I'm not saying that God doesn't want us to look our best. Of course He does! He wants us to take godly pride in ourselves because we are glorifying Him. But we can't shape our happiness on carnal things. Our happiness shouldn't depend and be built on things that only money can buy, but instead we should find complete satisfaction in the ONE thing money can't buy – SALVATION and an intimate relationship with Jesus Christ. Money can't buy the hunger that He fills and the thirst He alone quenches. Ask yourself, am I relying more on money than I am on God? Are you "praying for His answer" and "His will to be done" or are you trying to find it on your own?

WOO! I struggle deeply with the, 'if only' and the 'I wish' sayings. Struggles, where I constantly compare my intelligence, spiritual moments, and outer appearance with that of other Christians as well as those of the world. Jesus never tells us to doubt ourselves or Him! So, STOP it right here and right now and START watering confidence and drown out comparison!

"So, don't worry about these things, saying, "What will we eat? What will we drink? What will we wear? These things dominate the thoughts of unbelievers, but your heavenly Father already knows all your needs. Seek the Kingdom of God above all else, and live righteously, and he will give you everything you need.

- Matthew 6:31-33

Valleys, trials and defeat — oh my!

I love rainy weather. Why? I don't know. It just awakens something within me. I mean in reality we should embrace rainy days as well as the sunny days. Let's be real, we all know that every day will not be sunny. Therefore, I'm thankful for the rainy days. Rainy days are dreary and dark, but rain is one of the essential components for growth. Without rain, the sun would simply dry up the earth, ultimately killing everything including you and me. This applies to our spiritual life. If every day in our lives were sunny – we wouldn't need God for anything. We could do everything by our own power. I mean why pray when I've got everything I need, just the way I wanted. Why change when I'm perfect. BUT Jesus warned us that there WILL be trials and tribulations, but to take heart because He has overcome the world! (*John 16:33*). I believe that we go through our "rainy" season to allow God to do His growing within us. When we desire to develop our relationship with Christ, He has to cleanse us of some things and in order to cleanse us, He has to wash us and in order to wash us, He has to allow rain in our lives. Every now and then I believe God allows rainy days so that we don't forget who supplies the sun and the rain; those days where we have to consult Him constantly. Those days when He's our only light – our only source.

God, this is how I feel...

Writing down how I feel to God is one of the ways that I connect with Him. I love to write (as you can tell) and seeing my struggles on paper somehow makes the situation real. However, it doesn't stop there. On that same page, I write who God is to me and I list all of His attributes – He's my Savior, Friend, Way-maker, Healer, Protector, Comforter, Counselor and the list goes on and on because He is my EVERYTHING! In the beginning, you may find that taking time out of your busy schedule and actually writing to God is difficult. But *Dear*

Broken Girl, let me tell you, the first time you sit down and write out your struggles, battles, failures, fears, etc. AND then back it up with how amazing your Savior is.... whew! Words can't describe the feeling you will most likely experience - it's powerful! You're basically stating, "God, this is how I feel, and this is what I'm going through, but even though A through Z is going on in my life, You are still good! You are still on the throne! You ALWAYS have my best interest at hand and I will forever magnify Your Holy Name!" After praising God for who He is, I write one final thing down — a prayer of surrender. What am I surrendering to God? All of the things that I listed in the beginning of my note to Him. I continuously surrender to God everything that I am and all that I go through! He's a God who has anointed healing in His hands and the answer to all my problems as well as a plan for my life. This method can be used when you are sorrowful, but also when you're grateful!

Think about this:

- You cannot share in the Lord's glory without sharing in His suffering also!
- To be like Him is to love, live and suffer like Him!
- The battle is not yours, it's the Lord's
- You're not buried, you're planted... Now, bloom!

When you write down your current situation to God, and you totally surrender 'it' to Him by being open and honest; when you can still praise God in the midst of your storm, this is where your freedom begins – you just reached another level; a deeper level in Christ Jesus.

When you can praise God for who He is in spite of how you feel, or what you're going through or what you can or can't see; this is where your strength comes from! There's power in that. There's deliverance in that. There's **freedom** in that. *Don't* *waste your pain*, but instead find purpose and praise in the midst of it! Is this easy – no ma'am but the benefits are so worth it.

The Bible says that "the joy of the LORD is your strength" (*Nehemiah 8:10*). Therefore, the enemy knows that if he can deceive you into living down in the dumps and keep you depressed and stressed, you won't have the strength or the willpower to withstand his attacks. When you rejoice in the midst of your difficulties, you obtain victory over the enemy through Jesus!!

Don't waste your pain, but instead find purpose and praise in the midst of it

Without JOY you have no strength and without strength, you have no JOY

There's something so special about serving and trusting God especially when we can't "see" Him. I come to Him broken, but I leave whole or at least feeling a little stronger to fight in this battle called life! Brokenness + vulnerability + praise = wholeness in Christ. This is one of the many ingredients that the Lord uses to stir the pot of our hearts and honey, only He can make something GOOD out of it! Not only will He leave you satisfied, but others will be satisfied *through* you because you are being filled *in* Him.

Others will be satisfied through you because you are being filled in Him

Who's on the throne of your heart?

Your brokenness is welcomed here - but it doesn't stop here; He promises us that we will never be abandoned, destroyed or left in despair. Best of all, He also promises us His everlasting Kingdom!

Recently I lost intimacy with God. I felt the distance, but unfortunately, I couldn't *fix* the distance. But wait… we were never made to fix our own brokenness. That's why we serve a God whose desire for us is to make us whole. We should be willing to let our Savior (who exudes wholeness) put us back together piece by piece. I've placed things – such as comparison, Netflix, applause from others on the throne where only my Savior should reside.

When everything is ready, I will come and get you, so that you will always be with me where I am. - John 14:3

I've been saved since middle school, but lately, I've feared the eternal aspect of the next life with Christ. Why? Because I've treasured so much of this life and all its worldliness, such as my family and all that I desire to accomplish, that I have completely lost my focus. I've placed too much importance of my life on this side of eternity that I've completely overlooked the One who gives *true* life. I've doubted God to move in situations that seem like giants in my eyes; even when deep down I know that there is NOTHING too big for my God! *(Jer. 32:17)* I've doubted. I've wavered. I've wandered, but my God is still good! Tonight, as I'm writing this section of Dear Broken Girl, I'm totally surrendering the doubts, the wandering and the wavering over to Him. And I'm trusting Him to use this moment, this season, this experience to build me! To use me and my brokenness to help someone else. Who knows, perhaps that someone else is you.

I've placed Christ back on the throne where He so deservingly belongs. There are days where I open my Bible just to hug and experience a closeness with my Lord. I remember, one day opening my Bible and receiving this word from the Lord, **"God delights in those who are willing to be used by Him."** WOW! Here I am Lord, use me! (see *Isaiah 6:8*)

The bottom line is simply this - whether you're a new Christian, a seasoned Christian or you have not yet taken that step on the faith journey... at some point in your life, you will doubt God in some shape, form or fashion. But the Lord expects that; in fact, your doubt gives Him the opportunity to show Himself to be true! Be willing to be used by God in your 'this' moment. I promise you; the Lord won't let you down. He never has. He never will.

What do you need to water spiritually?

- spend more time with God
- listen to God rather than the world
- be real with yourself as well as others
- do acts of service for God to represent Him and only Him
- Set aside pride & pick up peace and forgiveness
- water confidence instead of comparison

Boy Crazy

I've mentioned in a previous chapter how my desire to have a man has decreased, and for the most part it has, *but* there are times where I am (two words): ***boy crazy!*** I mean it's so bad that a guy can simply look my way and I instantly hear wedding bells. And please don't let him start a conversation with *me* – BAM - we're married! It sounds funny and a bit pathetic, perhaps a bit scary, but I'm just being open and honest. And if truth be told, this happens a lot more often than you think with a lot of us. Although, most will not admit it. In real life, we become so consumed with a guy seeking us or dating us because we're so empty of the One who can truly fulfill us. Did you get that? Let me say it again, in real life we become so consumed with a guy seeking us or dating us because we're so empty of the One who can truly fulfill us! I've mentioned

Seek the King to shift your focus from being boy crazy to Jesus driven!

before, and I'll mention it again, it is okay to want a man to share life with. However, it's not okay to let your emotions override your reality. Because of my weakness when it comes to guys and my tendency to lose focus on Christ, I have accepted the fact that I am not ready for a relationship. I realize that I need to be filled by Him (Jesus) before I can get with him (a guy). Maybe you're like me, a bit boy crazy. I challenge you to find the reason behind your somewhat unhealthy need to have a guy in your life. Is it because you're extremely insecure about your appearance, talents, or worth? Seek the King to shift your focus from being boy crazy to Jesus driven!

Father,

Thank You for leading me to know that You alone can satisfy me. I pray that You shift my focus from being boy crazy to being Jesus-driven. I love You, Lord.

Amen.

Chapter 5

Willingness in the Waiting

Confidence in Christ will put your priorities into perspective, your purpose will be profound, and your confusion will be clarified.

Waiting on God

Have you ever waited on God? If so, have you waited patiently or impatiently? There's a song that my mema's church sings that says: "He may not come when you want Him – but He's always on time!" This is so true. I've waited on God many times, both patiently and impatiently, but you know what, each time God was ALWAYS on time – He has never failed me yet!

Mid-February 2018, my maternal mema became extremely ill. We were constantly in and out of the hospital and doctors' offices due to surgeries, check-ups, treatments, etc. I remembered when my mema first became ill, she stayed in the hospital for two and a half weeks! Those two and a half weeks turned our lives upside down. Throughout that tragic time, we found out that she had stage 5 chronic kidney disease. *Hearts broken. Tears shed. Prayers prayed. Praises spoken.* These four things summed up our entire battle. Little did we know that this battle would last for months and months... in fact, it's still ongoing. I begged God to save my grandmother's life; to reverse her kidney issues. There were nights where I wondered where the heck was God! Could He hear me? Was He there? It seemed like every night I would either soak mine or the hospital's pillows with my tears. When my words couldn't form, my wailing spoke for me (*Rom. 8:26* – "*And the Holy spirit helps us in our weakness. For example, we don't know what God wants us to pray for. But the Holy spirit prays for us with groanings that cannot be expressed in words*"). Within those seventeen days, my mema had to be revived once. Talk about a praying and broken time. Fast forward several months my mema is STILL ALIVE! I know this is only because of God's grace! We praised God for her good days while praying to God for more of those days. She still has Stage 5 kidney disease, but I believe that the same God that heard my cry and kept her alive is the same God that *if* it is His will, can reverse her disease. Nevertheless, just because He chose not to, I still choose to serve Him because

He is worthy. A lot of times, we give God an ultimatum…God if you heal, if you save, if you stop, if, if, if… *then* I'll serve you. No, no, no! I remember my Pastor saying one Sunday that if God doesn't do another thing for us, He is still worthy to be praised. Can I get an Amen?!

Even when I walk through the darkest valley, (the unknown), I will not be afraid - Ps. 23:4

The Lord has used my mema's life and her sufferings to prune the heart of many including hers, mine and my family's. Not even four months later, my paternal grandmother became extremely ill. She was hospitalized for over two months! There were so many times we thought she would not live to see another day. Her health decreased so drastically that we knew it would take a miracle to heal her! But how great is the King of kings and Lord of lords! *(On May 29, 2019 my grandmother won her battle against her illness and is now worshipping the King of kings in Heaven! RIP grandma Rochell.)*

Fast forward to December 19, 2018 - FIVE days before Christmas I found out that my dad had aggressive prostate cancer. I know God is a healer. How? He tells me in His Word that *by His stripes, we are healed.* (*Isaiah 53:5*) Yet even knowing this, it still hurts. I still have questions. And yes, some doubts. I still wonder why *my* daddy, God? But during my struggles, I've witnessed a strength in my dad that could only come from God. My dad said that this circumstance was well with his soul - and I believed his statement wholeheartedly. I praise God for that season of the unknown because it was during this time of waiting, blindly trusting God that showed me He is always an on-time God. He's a Deliverer and a Healer in His own way. I've learned that I must trust that He knows what's best for me and my family and stand on that. Not wavering but trusting His decisions. 2018 was a very tough year for my family, but you know what, God never left us once! Although we couldn't see it at the time, He had already prepared us for what was to come. We simply had to remain faithful to Him, trusting in Him and willing to step aside and allow His will to be done and as always, He remained faithful to us.

I've questioned God not only about these situations but so many other things. I think a lot of people are afraid to question God, but actually, I encourage you *to* question God. I promise you that the God who can calm the winds and the waves, the One who can raise a dead man to life with just His spoken word is *more* than capable and qualified to answer your questions! For my God is a powerful God! All creation shall bow down to Him! I don't know what you're going through right now or what's going on around you, but I want to tell you today that there is a Spirit within you that can direct your steps, comfort your heart and lead you to everlasting life! I serve a God who not only sees me in my struggles but sits with me during my struggles. So maybe you're like me, maybe you have a loved one battling cancer or an illness. Maybe it's you yourself struggling; I want to encourage you and let you know that you're not alone and that there is a Father who is in control and has all power and healing within His hands!

Father,

I thank You for using my situation to further Your kingdom. You will use this season in my life for Your glory and I believe You will be by my side through it all. I love You!

Amen.

Faithfulness

God is faithful! He shows His faithfulness time and time again. We just have to believe! *Dear Broken Girl,* what does He need to heal today for you? Only you can answer this question. Whatever it is, big or small, ask Him, trust Him and stand on the faithfulness that only He brings!

Over the years, God has been dealing with me spiritually. During my junior year of high school, God confirmed what He placed in my heart. I have attended my current school since first grade. One of the things He placed on my heart was to welcome first-year students to their new school. Towards the end of my junior year, I felt deep within my soul that this school needed a revival from the Lord. The more I grew in my faith, the more compelling I felt to actually take action. When the Lord first placed the desire in me to start a club at my school, my mind began to work overtime. I came up with where I was going to have the meeting, what would take place at these meetings, who was going to "volunteer" and I even came up with a name for the club. But this was all me. This was not what God wanted. I didn't take the time and consult God in depth before I started formulating all 'my' plans for what I thought God wanted and how to accomplish this task. But you better believe God put a stop to it right away and made His plan VERY plain. So after being disciplined by God, I readjusted myself. I prayed, fasted and invited other spiritually mature people to pray along with me. I wanted to make sure that what I was feeling was actually in His will for me and Neuse (my school).

Mind-blowing moment: I texted random people that popped into my head to pray with me about this calling that I felt the Lord had placed in my life. I gave no details. Just a vague message asking them to pray and fast. They all willingly and readily agreed. When I began to receive the confirmation texts, I remembered counting *twelve* responses. Hmmm, twelve responses - *Twelve* *disciples*.... get it? I was stunned, actually in awe of how the Lord had strategically placed twelve people on my heart to text. Twelve faithful believers in Christ took at least one minute out of their day for seven days to worship and pray to the King on my behalf. On the seventh day of our fasting and praying, the Lord revealed to me what His plans were for me. My response was, "Wait, Lord, you do know that I'm just a junior, right? I mean am I *really* ready for this? Am I spiritually ready for the Spirit to work in me, through me and around me?"

Those whom God calls – He qualifies!

Several months after much fasting and praying, God's plans began to unfold! I was approached out of the blue to lead a club called First Priority at our school. What is First Priority? It's a nationwide organization whose sole purpose is to bring Christ to school campuses. At our school, we met every Friday during study hall.

I can't tell you how much stress I had when I first took this project on. The devil was in my mind constantly – "nobody's going to show up; you can't speak in front of people; you're not popular like the other pretty girls… can't, can't, can't." I would doubt myself constantly. But God would send words of encouragement, volunteers to help, people with ideas and then there was my mom (always with a "you can do this baby because God's got this and you"). The first meeting we had *forty-six* students to attend! By week four our attendance had doubled and then some! My heart was overjoyed by the attendance especially because this consisted of students in *high school*! Not everyone who attended did so with the purpose of hearing about Christ, some came for the games, others for the food, but the bottom line is that they were ALL being introduced to Christ in some way. *Dear Broken Girl,* once I let go of my fears and put my trust and faith in God, it all came together. I had to realize that it's not about me. It's not in the number. God showed me that if only one person showed up weekly, His love is still being shared. That's what it's all about – always representing Christ well. Can we give God praise? For years, I waited and prayed for God's Word to be introduced to my fellow classmates and now, God in His own timing and in His own way has graced me with the opportunity to not only introduce Him but prayerfully lead others to everlasting life through Him! It just took total submission to Him.

"May He equip you with all you need for doing His will"- Heb. 13:21

I praise God for this because not only is His club known but it's flourishing and it's all for His Kingdom! So, whatever the Lord has placed on your heart, pray fervently for His clarification and praise Him in the process and most importantly seek and serve Him with all your heart!

what if you lived your purpose so greatly that other people would have the desire to find theirs

Goals

My main goal in life is to live for the King (being His forever servant). Another goal that I hold high is to remain true/loyal to my future husband. The others are just as important as the second one. As I've stated before one of my biggest life struggles is singleness. I would love to have someone special to cuddle, snuggle and laugh with. That special someone to share life's ups and downs with. Someone where our sole desire is to please our Lord and Savior, and by pleasing Christ, we please each other. But you know what, in the midst of my struggles, I have to trust and believe that *when* the time is right God and only God will send me that special someone that He has designed just for me. I've found that if I dwell on the fact that I don't have a boyfriend, I become a bit depressed and bitter. I have to fervently pray for God to get me out of this mood because remaining there could lead to an open door for the devil to come in and send me to the wrong someone! Not the someone destined to me by God but the someone designed to destroy me by Satan. **BUT** when I dwell on the promises of Jesus, I become more hopeful and content in this season that I am in! Jesus reminds me that during my season of waiting He's working on me. That I need to grow emotionally, spiritually, physically and even financially – but most importantly He reminds me that He's working in the same way with my future boo!

I've read a few books and stories about women who have surrendered their love life to the Father (which I believe we should all do). These women have surrendered totally to Christ to live a life for Him, that even if they were to remain single for the rest of their lives, they are content because they wholeheartedly trust the Lord. Yes, some of them have desires to be married, but not more than they desire a marriage of contentment and fulfillment between them and their heavenly Groom.

So, my question for you today, (and I'm asking myself the same question) if the Lord never gave you a boyfriend or husband, would it all be well with your soul? Would you still consider our Father as the *Good, Good Father* that we sing about? Will He still be the One you glorify? Could Jesus alone be your everything? That's a lot to take in and I've had heart-check after heart-check where I've had to be open and honest with not only myself but with God when answering these questions. As I grow in my faith my struggle has dwindled, not disappeared, but it's not as heavy on my heart as it was a year ago. Basically, what I'm trying to say is that there's nothing wrong with having a boyfriend, but I encourage you to become fully satisfied in who and Whose you are. Fully surrender your life to the King who holds today, tomorrow and forever.

Find beauty in Who has planted you and where
you are currently planted!

When we accept the reason for our wait (God's timing), it makes the waiting a bit easier to bear and might I say... enjoyable. Never would I want to hinder or forsake the blessings that the Lord has for me or even my future husband because I'm in the mood to cuddle right now. I'm not giving up on marriage; I'm aggressively diving into my heavenly marriage more. I so admire Jesus' love for me and if waiting reveals His pursuit and that love for me, well then, *I'll wait.*

My God,

Forgive me for placing man above You. Lord, right now I surrender my love life past, present and future to You. You are writing my story. So, right now Father I relinquish my desires to You, use them as You see fit. I love You, Lord.

Amen.

Choose a leader

I used to hate being a leader when I was younger. I did however, love being the line leader. (*Call me crazy, I know!*) I always thought being a leader was too much pressure, and to some extent it is because you have others looking and following you. So, I'm constantly repeating, "Don't screw up, Lexi. You're a leader now." Even in class when we did group projects, a leader had to be chosen, no matter what group I was placed in, nine times out of ten, I was chosen to be the leader. Why? I believe that it was because they saw something or better yet Someone in me that stood out from all the rest (or they just didn't want to do it, but I'm going to go with my first thought of why I was chosen). It wasn't my leadership skills that spoke volumes, but it was God working through me.

Now don't get me wrong, I didn't just jump at every opportunity to be a leader, there were times, that I didn't want to be the leader, because being a leader required responsibility. One of the things I wanted absolutely NOTHING to do with! I didn't want to fail my team. You and I both know that when a group fails, the blame is usually placed on the leader. Listen, we all have strengths and we all have weaknesses. In the Bible, God appointed leaders such as Adam, Moses, Joshua, Paul, David, and Esther, just to name a few. Were they perfect? No. Did they have it all together? No. Did they all willingly jump at the opportunity? No. *Dear Broken Girl*, God may be calling you to take on the role of leadership too. Will you answer the call?

Today I encourage you to be open to leadership, to step up to the challenge, big or small if this is God's calling for you. I encourage you to grip the hand of the Lord and JUST DO IT! For we are the head and not the tail. We are leaders, not followers. We are above and not beneath (*Deut. 28:13*). If God is calling you to step up and be a leader, then I challenge you to fulfill your leadership lifestyle TODAY!

A lot of people want
to get into a ministry position
You're already there –
the life you live is your ministry
All you have to do is get into position

Dear Future Husband

Due to my love of writing, I decided to write letters/notes to my future husband. I want him to know all about my good days as well as my bad days. I want to share special events in my life even special prayer requests I submitted on his behalf. I want to share information about my family and our struggles. I choose to write to him as if I'm talking to him face to face. It's like a diary, except it's not just for my special keeping, but actual letters I hope to one day give to my soulmate. Not only do I

Just because I haven't met him yet does not mean that I can't pray for him now.

keep him up to date about what I'm going through, I pray over him, his family, and our future. I speak truth over him in my writing. Just because I haven't met him yet does not mean that I can't pray for him now.

Writing these letters brings me a sense of peace. I made a vow to God, my dad and my future husband to remain pure. Which in and of itself has kept me from recklessly giving my heart and body to other guys. I have made mistakes; the sin of lust is a very powerful stronghold and easy to succumb to, but writing to my future reminds me that he is worth the wait. Unexplainable peace washes over me as I put the pen to paper and my heart beats for him with every word. I have these letters in individual envelopes kept in a special keepsake box to one day reveal to my future husband. I want him to read about all of my mistakes, accomplishments, miracles, and breakthroughs. I want him to know that even *then* I was praying for him.

I encourage you to write your thoughts and

prayers on paper whether it's to your future husband, your future self or your heavenly Father; write out your heart's desires and treasure those moments. Trusting and believing that God is reading them while preparing His answers for you.

Trust without borders

Then Elijah said to Ahab, "Go get something to eat and drink, for I hear a mighty rainstorm coming!" So Ahab went to eat and drink. But Elijah climbed to the top of Mount Carmel and bowed low to the ground and prayed with his face between his knees. Then he said to his servant, "Go and look out toward the sea." The servant went and looked, then returned to Elijah and said, "I didn't see anything." Seven times Elijah told him to go and look. Finally, the seventh time, his servant told him, "I saw a little cloud about the size of a man's hand rising from the sea." Then Elijah shouted, "Hurry to Ahab and tell him, 'Climb into your chariot and go back home. If you don't hurry, the rain will stop you!'" And soon the sky was black with clouds. A heavy wind brought a terrific rainstorm, and Ahab left quickly for Jezreel. Then the Lord gave special strength to Elijah.

- 1 Kings 18:41-46

This is a powerful story! Elijah shows us that his trust in God's promises brought about a reward. Think about this, Elijah told his servant that it was going to rain because God revealed it to him. In those days, there weren't meteorologists or weather apps, in fact there was not a cloud in the sky that day. Yet Elijah believed there was going to be a rainstorm! Elijah sent his servant out to look for a rain cloud SIX times and still he saw nothing! By his third time, I'm sure the servant began to think that Elijah was a bit crazy. Yet, he kept going back and back again. It was all about being obedient, faithful… trusting without borders! Do you see what

I see? Let me share what I get from this passage just in case! When God tells or promises us something, we may not see His results immediately. But we must stand firmly on our faith in God that He *always* delivers. If He said it, it will come to pass. In fact, you may not be able to see anything at all that's related to what you've been waiting or praying for, but just because you don't see it, doesn't mean that it's not happening, or shall I say — 'forming'. On the servants seventh trip to look at the sky, he saw a cloud the size of a man's hand the Bible says. The size may seem insignificant but think on this, it only takes faith the size of a mustard seed for miracles to happen. Maybe you've been going through this season for what seems like a million years and you keep experiencing the same thing – nothing. Or perhaps you're constantly coming up empty handed like the fishermen in the Bible. (*Luke 5:15*) Remember they caught no fish until the Lord spoke to them and THEN their boats couldn't even hold all the fish! Today, I encourage you to keep trusting, to keep waiting, to keep believing because if God said it, it will come to pass. "God, all I see is a little cloud" — and that, Dear Broken Girl, is all you need.

So now then....

We've talked about how being single should not be an empty, unfulfilled struggle, but rather a time where we can fully engage with the Father. I challenge you to be the girl who is not single and looking, but rather who is single and *still*.

He says, "Be still, and know that I am God...."

- Psalm 46:10

We are called *in this season* to be still in God's presence and to be moved in His timing. Oftentimes we miss the beauty behind being single because we're too focused on wishing we were dating. I'm preaching to myself right here. May I share something with you? When you dedicate your life to the only One who can satisfy you and fill the void of your heart, you will begin to see the blessings of being "alone".

for with God you are **never alone**

I have learned and am continuing to learn that dating Jesus is by far the best feeling to ever have. We [God and I] go to dinner, the movies, even ice cream dates - you name it! It's fun to date Jesus! Think about this: the One whom you sing praises to, receive the Holy Spirit from, receive endless love and grace, is the One you can date and hold hands with and there's no pressure, no judging, no compromising involved. Take comfort in knowing that you are not alone - when you're holding hands with the Father. You want to hold hands with someone? I encourage you to grab hold to our Father's hands.

Beautifully **BROKEN**... that's where God does His best work!

I remember one afternoon; I was laying in the backseat of my car looking up at the sky asking God to show Himself. To reveal Himself to me. To speak to me. I was struggling with giving Him my time. Time He so well deserved. I could actually feel the disconnect... so I asked Him to make Himself known in the clouds. And God did just that! See, in order for me to see the clouds moving – forming, I had to be still. The same applies to hearing from God. Sometimes we have to be still and just listen.

Dear Broken Girl...

It's amazing how we would trade everlasting water for temporary droplets. We think being in a relationship, getting money, wearing the best clothes, looking the best for him is better than surrendering *all* to Jesus. Oh how we have so blatantly misconstrued that this world is our home. Popularity is not your purpose. A spouse is not your source. A man cannot complete you. Money cannot buy you happiness. TRUE satisfaction is found in the open arms of our Father!! How dare we trade overflowing blessings for broken promises by broken people living broken lives! How dare we trade Christ's love for the world's lust! How dare we trade Jesus' truth for Satan's lies! May we remember that our Creator is far more valuable than the creations. May we hold onto the promises that He speaks, grace that He freely gives, and the love that He so willingly pours out for all of us! We are to walk on water with our eyes locked with our Maker NOT drowning in the lies of man. May we never trade eternity for temporary OR everlasting for emptiness OR truth for lies! May we never trade the ocean for droplets of water.

My purpose is to shine so bright that ALL the world can see the greatest Man that created you and me!

To the broken, He uses our brokenness and turns them into blessings! In our lowest moments, God shows us His ultimate strength. **(2 Cor. 12:9)**

To the lost, know that Jesus leaves the 99 to find you. You're never too far gone to come back home and you're never too lost to be found. **(Matt. 18:12)**

To the lonely, remember, you are not alone. In fact, the Word reminds us that in Christ we are never alone. Loneliness is real, but Dear Broken Girl, so is God. God is more real than you think and more present than you can ever imagine. Your loneliness is met with His presence and that is the beginning of wholeness. **(Deut. 31:6)**

Encouraging verses:

SINGLENESS:

- "Sometimes I wish everyone were single like me—a simpler life in many ways! But celibacy is not for everyone any more than marriage is. God gives the gift of the single life to some, the gift of the married life to others. I do, though, tell the unmarried and widows that singleness might well be the best thing for them, as it has been for me."
(1 Cor. 7:7-8 MSG)

- "And don't be wishing you were someplace else or with someone else. Where you are right now is God's place for you. Live and obey and love and believe right there. God, not your marital status, defines your life."
(1 Cor. 7:17 MSG)

- ♦ "And the single woman is focused on the things of the Lord so she can be holy both in body and spirit"

  (1 Cor. 7:34a TPT)

- ♦ "I am trying to help you and make things easier for you and not make things difficult, but so that you would have undistracted devotion, serving the Lord constantly with an undivided heart."

  (1 Cor. 7:35 TPT)

- ♦ "Make God the utmost delight and pleasure of your life, and he will provide for you what you desire the most."

  (Ps. 37:4 TPT)

- ♦ "You're only truly happy when you walk in total integrity, walking in the light of God's word. What joy overwhelms everyone who keeps the ways of God, those who seek him as their heart's passion!"

  (Ps. 119:1-2 TPT)

♦ "How can a young person stay pure? By obeying your word. I will study your commandments and reflect on your ways. I will delight in your decrees and not forget your word."
(Ps. 119:9,15-16 NLT)

DEPRESSION/ANXIETY/FEAR:

♦ "So keep your thoughts *continually* fixed on all that is authentic and real, honorable and admirable, beautiful and respectful, pure and holy, merciful and kind. And fasten your thoughts on every glorious work of God, praising him *always*."
(Phil.4:8 TPT)

♦ "The Lord hears his people when they call to him for help. He rescues them from all their troubles. The Lord is close to the brokenhearted; he rescues those whose spirits are crushed."
(Ps. 34:17-18 NLT)

♦ "So I say to my soul, "Don't be discouraged. Don't be disturbed. For I know my God will break through for me." Then I'll have plenty of reasons to praise him all over again. Yes, living before his face is my saving grace!"

(Ps. 42:11 TPT)

♦ "And everything I've taught you is so that the peace which is in me will be in you and will give you great confidence as you rest in me. For in this unbelieving world you will experience trouble and sorrows, but you must be courageous, for I have conquered the world!"

(John 16:33 TPT)

♦ "For God has not given us a spirit of fear and timidity, but of power, love, and self-discipline."

(2 Timothy 1:7 NLT)

♦ "Don't panic. I'm with you. There's no need to fear for I'm your God. I'll give you strength. I'll help you. I'll hold you steady, keep a firm grip on you."

(Is. 41:10 MSG)

♦ "This is my command—be strong and courageous! Do not be afraid or discouraged. For the Lord your God is with you wherever you go."

(Joshua 1:9 NLT)

INSECURITY/BEAUTY:

♦ "What matters is not your outer appearance—the styling of your hair, the jewelry you wear, the cut of your clothes—but your inner disposition. Cultivate inner beauty, the gentle, gracious kind that God delights in."

(1 Pet. 3:3-4 MSG)

♦ "Therefore we do not become discouraged [spiritless, disappointed, or afraid]. Though our outer self is [progressively] wasting away, yet our inner *self* is being [progressively] renewed day by day."

(2 Cor. 4:16 AMP)

♦ "For we are God's masterpiece. He has created us anew in Christ Jesus, so we can do the good things he planned for us long ago." **(Eph. 2:10 NLT)**

♦ "Oh yes, you shaped me first inside, then out; you formed me in my mother's womb. I thank you, High God—you're breathtaking! Body and soul, I am marvelously made! I worship in adoration—what a creation! You know me inside and out, you know every bone in my body; You know exactly how I was made, bit by bit, how I was sculpted from nothing into something. Like an open book, you watched me grow from conception to birth; all the stages of my life were spread out before you, The days of my life all prepared before I'd even lived one day."

(Ps. 139: 13-16 MSG)

⬥ "You're beautiful from head to toe, my dear love, beautiful beyond compare, absolutely flawless."

(SOS 4:7 MSG)

FOLLOWING JESUS:

⬥ "Then Jesus went to work on his disciples. "Anyone who intends to come with me has to let me lead. You're not in the driver's seat; *I* am."

(Matt. 16:24 MSG)

⬥ "Imitate me, just as I *imitate* Christ."

(1 Cor. 11:1 AMP)

⬥ "For God called you to do good, even if it means suffering, just as Christ suffered for you. He is your example, and you must follow in his steps."

(1 Pet. 2:21 NLT)

- Then Jesus said, "I am light to the world and those who embrace me will experience life-giving light, and they will never walk in darkness." **(John 8:12 TPT)**

- My sheep listen to my voice; I know them, and they follow me. **(John 10:27 NLT)**

- So you must live as God's obedient children. Don't slip back into your old ways of living to satisfy your own desires. You didn't know any better then. But now you must be holy in everything you do, just as God who chose you is holy. For the Scriptures say, "You must be holy because I am holy." **(1 Pet. 1:14-16 NLT)**

- Yes, I am the vine; you are the branches. Those who remain in me, and I in them, will produce much fruit. For apart from me you can do nothing. Anyone who does not remain in me is thrown away like a useless branch and withers. Such branches are gathered into a pile to be burned. But if you remain in me and my words remain in you, you may ask for anything you want, and it will be granted! When you produce much fruit, you are my true disciples. This brings great glory to my Father. **(John 15:5-8 NLT)**

ANGER:

♦ Understand this, my dear brothers and sisters: You must all be quick to listen, slow to speak, and slow to get angry. Human anger does not produce the righteousness God desires.

   (James 1:19-20 NLT)

♦ Fools vent their anger, but the wise quietly hold it back. **(Prov. 29:11 NLT)**

- Hot tempers start fights; a calm, cool spirit keeps the peace. **(Prov. 15:18 MSG)**

- Hatred stirs up conflict, but love covers over all wrongs. **(Prov. 10:12 NIV)**

- Because human anger does not produce the righteousness that God desires. **(James 1:20 NLT)**

- But now rid yourselves [completely] of all these things: anger, rage, malice, slander, and obscene (abusive, filthy, vulgar) language from your mouth. **(Col. 3:8 AMP)**

- Words kill, words give life; they're either poison or fruit—you choose. **(Prov. 18:21 MSG)**

- Stop being angry! Turn from your rage! Do not lose your temper— it only leads to harm. For the wicked will be destroyed, but those who trust in the Lord will possess the land. **(Ps. 37:8 NLT)**

PURPOSE:

- Stop imitating the ideals and opinions of the culture around you, but be inwardly transformed by the Holy Spirit through a total reformation of how you think. This will empower you to discern God's will as you live a beautiful life, satisfying and perfect in his eyes. **(Rom. 12:2 TPT)**

- Now go *in my authority* and make disciples of all nations, baptizing them in the name of the Father, the Son, and the Holy Spirit. And teach them to faithfully follow all that I have commanded you. And never forget that I am with you every day, even to the completion of this age." **(Matt. 28:19-20 TPT)**

- So whether you eat or drink, or whatever you do, do it all for the glory of God. **(1 Cor. 10:31 NLT)**

- "You are the salt of the earth; but if the salt has lost its taste (purpose), how can it be made salty? It is no longer good for anything, but to be thrown out and walked on by people [when the walkways are wet and slippery]. "You are the light of [Christ to] the world. A city set on a hill cannot be hidden; nor does *anyone* light a lamp and put it under a basket, but on a lampstand, and it gives light to all who are in the house. Let your light shine before men in such a way that they may see your good deeds *and* moral excellence, and [recognize and honor and] glorify your Father who is in heaven. **(Matt. 5:13-16 AMP)**

⬥ And so, dear brothers and sisters, I plead with you to give your bodies to God because of all he has done for you. Let them be a living and holy sacrifice—the kind he will find acceptable. This is truly the way to worship him. Don't copy the behavior and customs of this world, but let God transform you into a new person by changing the way you think. Then you will learn to know God's will for you, which is good and pleasing and perfect. Because of the privilege and authority God has given me, I give each of you this warning: Don't think you are better than you really are. Be honest in your evaluation of yourselves, measuring yourselves by the faith God has given us. Just as our bodies have many parts and each part has a special function, so it is with Christ's body. We are many parts of one body, and we all belong to each other. **(Rom. 12:1-5 NLT)**

♦ You are to love the Lord Yahweh, your God, with every passion of your heart, with all the energy of your being, with every thought that is within you, and with all your strength. This is the great and supreme commandment. And the second is this: 'You must love your neighbor in the same way you love yourself.' You will never find a greater commandment than these." **(Mark 12:30-31 TPT)**

BROKEN/EMPTINESS:

● Then Jesus said, "Come to me, all of you who are weary and carry heavy burdens, and I will give you rest. Take my yoke upon you. Let me teach you, because I am humble and gentle at heart, and you will find rest for your souls. For my yoke is easy to bear, and the burden I give you is light." **(Matt. 11:28-30 NLT)**

● But he answered me, "My grace is always more than enough for you, and my power finds its full expression through your weakness." So I will celebrate my weaknesses, for when I'm weak I sense more deeply the mighty power of Christ living in me. So I'm *not defeated* by my weakness, but delighted! For when I feel my weakness and endure mistreatment—when I'm surrounded with troubles on every side and face persecution *because of my love* for Christ—I am made yet stronger. For my weakness becomes a portal to God's power. **(2 Cor. 12:9-10 TPT)**

- If your heart is broken, you'll find God right there; if you're kicked in the gut, he'll help you catch your breath. **(Ps. 34:18 MSG)**

- He heals the wounds of every shattered heart. **(Ps. 147:3 TPT)**

- Keep *actively* watching and praying that you may not come into temptation; the spirit is willing, but the body is weak. **(Matt. 26:41 AMP)**

ABOUT THE AUTHOR

Alexis (Lexi) Monet Howell, is a native of Johnston County. She is a 2019 high school graduate of Neuse Charter School (Smithfield, NC). Lexi is best known by her passion for reaching the broken and is using that connection to show everyone a God who breathes wholeness. Alexis embodies the character of a young woman whose soul is on fire to pursue Jesus wholeheartedly! She has been called by God as a spiritual mentor to young girls, teens, and ladies whose future is clouded by the cares of the world. Lexi is a small-town girl with a big-time heart! She is passionate about the Lord's people and is willing to do all that she can to lead them to the One who radically changed her life!

Alexis is in the process of writing her next book, Never Alone.

THANK YOU!!!

Dear Broken Girl, thank you SO much for reading my first book!! I pray you were encouraged by it! Please know that I am praying over and with you! You are loved beyond comprehension. You are seen even when you hide. And you are known by the Creator of the Universe.

I welcome contact from my readers! You can contact me via email: ahowell408@gmail.com or follow me (*Dear Broken Girl*) on social media (Instagram, Twitter, and Facebook)!

Xoxo,

Lexi Howell

Father,

I want to say thank You for simply being You.
For being a God who loves, but also the One who
can speak life and true identity over Your
children. Help me to remember that I am
royalty! You are my King. Thank You for speaking
to and over me.

I love You, Lord.

Amen.

Made in the USA
Columbia, SC
23 June 2019